A Practitioner's Guide to INNOCENT SPOUSE RELIEF

Proven Strategies for Winning Section 6015 Tax Cases

Third Edition

By Christine S. Speidel and Audrey Patten

AMERICAN BAR ASSOCIATION
Tax Section

The views and opinions expressed herein are entirely those of the author. Nothing contained herein is to be considered as the rendering of legal advice, nor should it be construed as representing the opinions, views, or actions of the American Bar Association or the Section of Taxation, unless duly approved by the Association or the Section. This book is intended for educational and informational purposes only.

The views expressed herein have not been approved by the House of Delegates nor the Board of Governors, nor the Section of Taxation of the American Bar Association and, accordingly, should not be construed as representing the policy of the American Bar Association.

Printed in the United States of America.

Published by the American Bar Association Section of Taxation,1050 Connecticut Ave. NW, Suite 400, Washington, DC 20036; www.americanbar.org/tax.

13-Digit ISBN: 978-1-63905-149-6 (Print)

13 Digit ISBN: 978-1-63905-150-2 (E-book)

For more information, contact the ABA Service Center at (800) 285-2221 and mention product code 5470838 or visit www.ShopABA.org.

Table of Contents

About the Authors

Christine S. Speidel is an Assistant Professor and Director of the Federal Tax Clinic at Villanova University Charles Widger School of Law. Until her appointment at Villanova, Ms. Speidel practiced law at Vermont Legal Aid. She initially focused on representing domestic violence survivors in family court matters, and also practiced in the areas of public benefits, health care, and tax while at Vermont Legal Aid. Ms. Speidel served on the Family Rules Committee of the Vermont Supreme Court from 2008 to 2018.

Over the past 14 years Ms. Speidel has represented hundreds of low-income individuals in a wide variety of IRS controversy and collection matters. As a member and leader of the ABA Section of Taxation Pro Bono and Tax Clinics Committee, she has participated in multiple comment projects and other efforts to highlight the impact of tax policy and administration issues on low-income individuals and particularly on survivors of domestic violence.

Audrey Patten is a Lecturer on Law and Clinical Instructor at the Legal Services Center of Harvard Law School's Tax Clinic. Her practice focuses on representing low-income clients in cases and controversies before the Internal Revenue Service, the United States Tax Court, and the Massachusetts Department of Revenue. In addition, she litigates tax cases in the United States District and Circuit Courts.

Prior to joining the Tax Clinic, Ms. Patten was an attorney in Harvard's Consumer Protection Clinic, in which she represented domestic violence survivors in debt collections, bankruptcy, and affirmative consumer protection cases as part of a medical-legal partnership with the Passageway Domestic Abuse and Intervention Program at Brigham and Women's Hospital. Ms. Patten began her legal career as a staff attorney in the Battered Women's Legal Assistance Project/Family Law Unit at Merrimack Valley Legal Services in Lowell, MA.

Foreword

One of my favorite quotations in the history of tax is from Justice Benjamin Cardozo, noting, "Life in all its fullness must supply the answer to the riddle" of statutory language.[1] The opinion from which it is extracted has come under criticism, including feminist criticism.[2] But for anyone working in the field of tax controversy, it is hard to escape the sense that tax law, far from being a dry, static practice, actually requires the practitioner to not only know the law but also know something about the vagaries of human existence.

This is especially true for one of the foundational building blocks of the individual income tax, namely, the taxable unit. In many countries, the income tax is applied to the individual taxpayer. Not so the United States: Its Internal Revenue Code recognizes both a single taxpayer, a marital unit filing jointly, and a marital unit filing separately (as well as head of household filing status). The treatment of a married taxpayer as different from a single individual brings all sorts of complications—including when a married taxpayer will be considered not married under the Code. But the introduction of joint and several liability exponentially ramps up the

---

[1] Welch v. Helvering, 290 U.S. 111, 115 (1933).

[2] *See, e.g.*, Mary Louise Fellows, *Welch v. Helvering*, in FEMINIST JUDGEMENTS: REWRITTEN TAX OPINIONS 103 (Bridget J. Crawford and Anthony C. Infanti eds., 2017); Ajay K. Mehrota, *'Life in All Its Fullness': Cardozo, Fellows, and the Critical Context of* Welch v. Helvering, 151 PITTSBURGH TAX REVIEW 15 (2019).

complexity and consequences of filing jointly with one's spouse. Add in the power imbalance that exists in many marital relationships, and you have an environment rife with inequitable outcomes.

Congress recognized the seriousness of these consequences and tried on several occasions to address them, short of repealing joint and several liability.[3] As discussed in Chapter 1 of this guide, Congress legislated in 1971, and again in 1984, creating an equitable relief provision known colloquially as "innocent spouse." It legislated again in 1998, with the Senate holding a separate hearing on the issue, with two panels, one of spouses who had been denied relief under the current law, and one of experts.[4]

As this book shows, I.R.C. § 6015 as enacted in 1998 still would require much clarification by the IRS and the courts, along with several legislative amendments, and we aren't done with it yet. That's where Christine Speidel and Audrey Patten come in, updating Robert Nadler's *Practitioner's Guide to Innocent Spouse Relief* and providing a roadmap through the decision to file jointly (Chapter 2), the legislative language and courts' interpretation of that language (Chapters 3 to 6), including community property issues (Chapter 7). The authors then move to practical advice, covering the administrative process (Chapter 9), the stages of petitioning and trial in the Tax Court (Chapters 10 through 12), obtaining a refund (Chapter 13), and on to a discussion of other collection alternatives, should the taxpayer be denied relief from joint and several liability (Chapter 14). The final chapter (Chapter 15) has a helpful state-by-state summary of state innocent spouse relief. Throughout, the authors point out areas that are still unsettled and suggest possible approaches. They highlight how the specific facts of the taxpayer's situation, including physical, emotional, or financial marital abuse, can tip the scale toward or away from relief. The discussion in Chapter 8 about meeting the client and building the case for relief demonstrates this point.

Who will benefit from this book? Anyone, really, who has an interest in the way law approaches marital property and taxes. It will be an invaluable guide to practitioners who concentrate on tax controversy practice; it will also guide the family law practitioner whose clients may face tax liabilities; it will be a refresher for academics and students alike on the current state of the law relating to I.R.C. sections 6015 and 66. It is a fascinating read, richly illustrated with stories (cases) of how the tax code, the Internal

---

[3] In 2001 and again in 2005, I recommended that Congress repeal I.R.C. 6013(d) (joint and several liability) and legislatively overrule Poe v. Seaborn, 282 U.S. 101 (1930). *See* National Taxpayer Advocate 2001 Annual Report to Congress 128 and National Taxpayer Advocate 2005 Annual Report to Congress 407.

[4] *IRS Restructuring (Innocent Spouse Rules): Hearing on H.R. 2676 Before the Sen. Comm. On Finance*, 105th Cong. 529 (1998).

Revenue Service, and the courts deal with the "fullness" of married (or formerly married) taxpayers' tax debts. While it does not solve the riddle for every case, it gives us many helpful clues to achieve the best possible resolution of a troubling and built-in problem with our tax law. I am grateful to Christine and Audrey for undertaking this update.

Nina E. Olson
Executive Director, Center for Taxpayer Rights
(National Taxpayer Advocate, 2001–2019)
March 2022
Washington, DC

Preface

Since the second edition of this book was published in 2014, we have seen important case law and administrative developments in the wake of Rev. Proc. 2013-34 as well as legislative changes to Section 6015 of the Internal Revenue Code. The third edition updates and expands the original editions written by Robert B. Nadler. It incorporates updates in the Code, Tax Court and United States Circuit Court case law, and IRS practices, and alerts readers to unresolved issues likely to be litigated over the coming years under the Taxpayer First Act of 2019.

This edition also offers a significant amount of new material, with three new chapters and substantial revisions to others.

- Chapter 8, "Meeting Your Client," provides expanded information and practical tips for successfully communicating a client's full circumstances to the IRS, including translating state law terms and proving spousal abuse.
- The chapter on tax court jurisdiction has become "Judicial Fora," expanding the book beyond the U.S. Tax Court and describing the possibilities for obtaining relief in other federal courts.
- A new chapter focused on community property states addresses the intersection of community property taxation and relief under I.R.C. § 6015, and also guides the practitioner through relief from community property taxation under I.R.C. § 66.

- Recognizing that an increasing number of states have adopted procedures for spousal relief from state tax liabilities, we have added a chapter summarizing relief available at the state level to provide a starting point for practitioners.
- A chapter on collection alternatives rounds out the trio of new chapters and renders the book a more comprehensive resource.

It was an honor to write the third edition, and we hope that you find this book as useful as we have found the previous editions. We are deeply indebted to Robert B. Nadler, not only for his research and writing, but also for his leadership on innocent spouse issues nationally. This book is a revision of the second edition, of which Bob was the sole author. We have embraced Bob's approach to the material, aiming to provide a concise, user-friendly guide that explains the law but also the practical realities of representing taxpayers in spousal relief cases.

We would like to thank the many people who helped bring this edition to fruition. Melinda Dunmire, Benjamin Fidalgo, Ramón Ortiz, Nancy Ryan, and David Sams consulted on state relief options. Nina Olson and Mandi Matlock gave valuable comments on IRS practices, and Cate Hillin and Shuyu Sun provided helpful research assistance. We are grateful for the excellent ABA Tax Section publishing staff who supported this book, Todd Reitzel and Greg Peacock. Finally, we would also like to recognize Mary Michelle Gillum, Keith Fogg, Susan Morgenstern, Nina Olson, and Carlton Smith for their work on innocent spouse issues nationally and their ongoing advice. Their dedicated and creative advocacy has measurably improved the fairness of the tax system.

Christine S. Speidel and Audrey Patten
April 2022

Chapter 1: Innocent Spouse Relief—Introduction and History

I. Introduction

Married Filing Jointly is the preferred personal income tax status for most married couples. It is the unique status that allows two individuals to file together, and thereby combine their possibilities for deductions and credits. However, it also binds both spouses to joint and several liability, regardless of which spouse's income generated more tax liability. Because this can lead to harsh results, there is the possibility to obtain relief. Relief from joint and several liability is available through § 6015 of the Internal Revenue Code ("I.R.C."). Relief under § 6015 is commonly referred to as "spousal relief" or "innocent spouse relief."[1]

Versions of innocent spouse relief have existed in the Internal Revenue Code since 1971. The current law, I.R.C. § 6015, provides the most expansive opportunities for relief to date and was enacted through the IRS Restructuring and Reform Act of 1998. The major innovation of the 1998 changes was providing for equitable relief in I.R.C. § 6015(f). This is one of the only sections in the entire Code that explicitly states the IRS

---

[1] Throughout the text, the terms "spousal relief," "innocent spouse relief," and "§ 6015 relief" will be used interchangeably.

may weigh a taxpayer's individual facts and circumstances when deciding whether to grant relief.[2]

Upon its passage, I.R.C. § 6015 raised several major legal questions that resulted in years of litigation in the United States Tax Court and in the circuit courts. There were three initial issues that generated ongoing litigation in the first decade after § 6015's passage. First, the IRS disputed whether judicial review was available in equitable relief cases, arguing that the Tax Court did not have jurisdiction. Second, the IRS and taxpayers disputed the scope of evidence admissible in the Tax Court, and the Tax Court's standard of review. Finally, the IRS attempted to limit the time to bring equitable relief claims under § 6015(f) to two years from the commencement of IRS collection activity for the tax year at issue.

Recently, the Taxpayer First Act amended § 6015, codifying the Court's standard and scope of review. There is currently a new era of innocent spouse litigation opening as taxpayers, the IRS, and the courts interpret the new statutory language.

II. History of Innocent Spouse Relief

While joint and several liability and innocent spouse relief are closely related legal concepts, their histories are to a great extent different. Prior to 1918, married couples were not allowed to file joint returns. In 1918, Congress enacted a law allowing married taxpayers to file joint income tax returns.[3] In 1921, Congress clarified the law to provide that the tax on a joint return was to be computed on aggregate income.[4] With the introduction of joint returns, the IRS took the position that each spouse was jointly and severally liable for all the tax owed on the return. Joint and several liability allowed the IRS to collect on taxes owed from either spouse without regard to which spouse earned the income. Several federal courts ruled against the IRS's position,[5] but in 1938 Congress imposed joint and several liability on joint filers.[6] The 1938 law did not provide any relief for situations where one spouse had no knowledge of the other spouse's omission of income on the joint return. The only option for a spouse to escape joint liability was to prove that they had been forced to sign the return under duress.

---

[2] Another code section with a provision for equitable relief is I.R.C. § 6511(h), known as the "financial disability" provision.

[3] Revenue Act of 1918, § 223, 40 Stat. 1057, 1074.

[4] *See* Revenue Act of 1921, § 223(b)(2), 42 Stat. 227, 250. For a good discussion of the history of innocent spouse relief, especially the legislative history, see Bryan T. Camp, *The Unhappy Marriage of Law and Equity in Joint Return Liability*, 108 Tax Notes 1307 (2005).

[5] Cole v. Comm'r, 81 F.2d 485 (9th Cir. 1935).

[6] *See* Revenue Act of 1938, § 51(b), 52 Stat. 447, 476.

For the next 33 years, no version of innocent spouse relief was available. During that time, it became increasingly apparent that joint and several liability produced very harsh results for some innocent spouses.[7] Congress thus passed a limited version of innocent spouse relief in 1971, codified as I.R.C. § 6013(e).[8]

III. IRS Restructuring and Reform Act of 1998

In 1998, Congress passed the IRS Restructuring and Reform Act of 1998, part of which expanded innocent spouse relief.[9] Newly enacted § 6015, the law in effect today, provides three distinct types of relief. First, § 6015(b) provides relief similar to the original relief provided in § 6013(e), which was repealed. Second, § 6015(c) provides relief to taxpayers who were divorced, legally separated, or had been living apart for more than 12 months. I.R.C. § 6015(b) and (c) provide relief only in cases involving an understatement of tax, also called a deficiency. A tax deficiency means the return fails to account for all the taxpayers' income. These sections do not provide relief for situations in which the taxpayers stated all their liability correctly but then failed to pay the full amount owed.[10] The third type of relief is in § 6015(f). I.R.C. § 6015(f) provided a new form of relief, equitable relief, which is available in both understatement and underpayment cases. Equitable relief is only available when relief is not available under subsection (b) or (c), meaning a taxpayer cannot select § 6015(f) relief if they were already qualified under § 6015(b) or (c).[11]

As part of the new law, Congress also provided for innocent spouse relief in community property states under I.R.C. § 66(c). The basic concept of "community property" is that property acquired during the marriage automatically becomes the joint property of the marriage, and then gets divided equally upon divorce.[12] The exact form of community property law and division is subject to variations in state law. In general, federal law does not supersede state community property laws when determining

---

[7] *See* Scudder v. Comm'r, 48 T.C. 36, 41 (1967).

[8] Act of Jan. 12, 1971, Pub. L. No. 91-679, § 1, 84 Stat. 2063 (formerly codified at I.R.C. § 6013(e) before repeal).

[9] I.R.S. Restructuring and Reform Act of 1998, Pub. L. No. 105-206, § 3201(a), 112 Stat. 685, 734 (codified at I.R.C. § 6015, repealing and replacing § 6013(e)).

[10] A "deficiency" in income taxes is defined at I.R.C. § 6211. Sometimes a case hinges on whether a deficiency was involved. For example, if the amount in controversy resulted from an overstatement of withheld taxes, section 6213(b) would allow immediate assessment of the amount as a math error. In such case, the taxpayer might not have the right to claim innocent spouse relief under sections 6015(b) and (c), because there was no deficiency asserted. *See* Schwind v. Comm'r, T.C. Summ. Op. 2008-119.

[11] I.R.C. § 6015(f)(2).

[12] Mansell v. Mansell, 490 U.S. 581, 584 (1993).

ownership of a given asset.[13] The assets of each partner acquired during the marriage are, by operation of law, joint assets of the marriage, including those generating tax. I.R.C. § 66(c) provides for traditional relief and equitable relief. Traditional relief under § 66(c) requires that no joint return was filed, that an item of community income property was not included in the gross income of the requesting spouse, the requesting spouse did not know or have reason to know of the community income, and taking into account all the facts and circumstances, it is inequitable to include the community income in the requesting spouse's gross income.

IV. Innocent Spouse Relief Enters an Era of Intense Litigation

After the passage of § 6015, the IRS took positions that tried to hold back the new law's expansive effect. For example, the IRS immediately began arguing that the Tax Court did not have the authority to review any denials of equitable relief by the IRS. Another point of contention was the extent to which new evidence could be admitted in Tax Court litigation, with the IRS arguing that evidence had to be limited to the administrative record already submitted to the agency. The statute of limitations for bringing claims also generated litigation. All of these controversies eventually resulted in Congress weighing in with changes in the law.

A. Jurisdiction of the Tax Court over Section 6015(f) Equitable Relief

To claim spousal relief as a standalone claim, taxpayers must first apply directly to the IRS unless the claim is made in a deficiency petition. I.R.C. § 6015(e) allows the requesting spouse to file a petition for relief in the United States Tax Court for review of an IRS determination under any subsection of § 6015, after the taxpayer receives a final determination from the IRS on their § 6015 claim or after the passage of six months since applying, whichever is sooner.

Before § 6015(e) was amended in 2006, the IRS' position was that the Tax Court did not have statutory authority to review denials of § 6015(f) equitable relief. A seminal case on this issue was *Butler v. Commissioner*.[14] In *Butler*, the taxpayer asked the Tax Court to review a denial of relief under § 6015(f) in the context of a deficiency proceeding. The IRS argued that § 6015(e) did not provide jurisdictional authority to the Tax Court to review denials of equitable relief. The Tax Court disagreed with the

---

[13] Powell v. Comm'r, 101 T.C. 489, 494 (1993) ("Because domestic relations are preeminently matters of state law, we have consistently recognized that Congress, when it passes general legislation, rarely intends to displace state authority in this area.") *quoting* Mansell 490 U.S. at 587.

[14] Butler v. Comm'r, 114 T.C. 276 (2000).

IRS and held that it had jurisdiction as part of its traditional authority to redetermine a proposed deficiency.

Later that same year, *Fernandez v. Commissioner* dealt with the jurisdiction question in the context of a "standalone" § 6015(e) relief petition, i.e. a petition filed without any other basis for Tax Court jurisdiction.[15] The IRS filed a motion to dismiss the taxpayer's claim for relief under § 6015(f). The Tax Court held that Congress intended the Court to have jurisdiction to determine appropriate relief in controversies involving the denial of relief under all three subsections of § 6015.

Then, in *Ewing v. Commissioner* (*Ewing I*),[16] the IRS moved to dismiss the taxpayer's standalone petition for review of the denial of equitable relief in a case which involved only an underpayment in tax. The Tax Court held that not only did it have jurisdiction to review a denial of relief in understatement cases, those involving deficiencies, but it had jurisdiction in cases involving underpayments. In 2006, the Court of Appeals for the Ninth Circuit agreed with the IRS, reversing the Tax Court, and held that the Tax Court did not have jurisdiction under § 6015(e) unless the liability arose from a deficiency.[17]

In late 2006, Congress responded to the *Ewing* decision by amending § 6015(e) to provide the Tax Court with authority to review all denials of equitable relief.[18]

B. Scope of Evidence and Standard of Review

The current state of the law is that, while the standard of review in standalone innocent spouse cases filed in the Tax Court after an IRS Notice of Final Determination is *de novo*, the taxpayer is limited to presenting evidence that is contained in the IRS's administrative file, plus any newly discovered or previously unavailable evidence. It is still an open question as to whether this limitation applies to other contexts, such as when § 6015 relief is raised in a deficiency proceeding.[19] This "administrative record rule" as applied to innocent spouse proceedings has a disputed recent history.

In standalone § 6015 cases brought before the Tax Court, the IRS consistently argued that the Court could only consider information that was

---

[15] Fernandez v. Comm'r, 114 T.C. 324 (2000).

[16] Ewing v. Comm'r, 118 T.C. 494 (2002), *rev'd, Ewing III*, 439 F.3d 1009 (9th Cir. 2006).

[17] *See* Ewing III, 439 F.3d at 1009, *vacating Ewing II*, 122 T.C. 32 (2004) *and rev'g Ewing I*, 118 T.C. 494 (2002).

[18] *See* Tax Relief and Health Care Act of 2006 (TRHCA), Pub. L. No. 109-432, div. C, § 408(a), 120 Stat. 2922, 3061 (amending I.R.C. § 6015).

[19] There is an argument that the administrative record rule should not apply if the IRS has not made a determination at the time the Tax Court petition is filed, both under the plain language of § 6015(e)(7) and because at that point there would not be a meaningful administrative record for the Court to review.

included in the administrative record.[20] The administrative record consists of the evidence submitted to the IRS at the time the agency was reviewing the taxpayer's application for administrative relief. The Tax Court has taken the position generally that "[a]bsent a showing made with clear evidence to the contrary, an agency is presumed to have properly designated the administrative record."[21] The presence of an "administrative record rule" therefore puts the onus on a Tax Court petitioner that any evidence they wish to introduce was either properly before the IRS at the time of the administrative review of their innocent spouse claim or that it was not available at the time of the claim. The rule can particularly harm taxpayers with limited resources or education because they may be unable to provide complete information during the administrative process for various reasons, including language barriers, inability to take time off from work to gather records, and lack of understanding of the tax laws.

Many unrepresented taxpayers do not understand what types of records should be submitted during the administrative proceedings. In situations where domestic abuse was present in the relationship, the requesting spouse may not have access to the nonrequesting spouses' records.[22] In addition, some taxpayers have difficulty taking time off from work to locate records and others have language barriers that prevent understanding what records are necessary.

The Tax Court ruled in *Ewing v. Commissioner* (*Ewing II*)[23] that a trial in Tax Court was a *de novo* proceeding and it could consider new matters raised at trial that were not included in the administrative record. It later affirmed this position in *Porter v. Commissioner* (*Porter I*).[24] As described in Section VI below, the Taxpayer First Act has effectively rolled back the Tax Court's position and brought the administrative record rule back into force.

C. *The Statute of Limitations in Equitable Relief Cases*

The statute of limitations in § 6015(f) equitable relief cases also generated a string of court battles. The normal statute of limitations for the collection

---

[20] The IRS also argued that its equitable relief determinations should be reviewed for abuse of discretion. *See, e.g.*, Wilson v. Comm'r, 705 F.3d 980 (9th Cir. 2013), *aff'g* T.C. Memo. 2010-134 (A.O.D. 2012-07, 2013-25 I.R.B. 2013-25 (June 17, 2013)). After it lost the Wilson case, the IRS in an Action on Decision abandoned the argument that the Tax Court should review equitable relief cases for an abuse of discretion.

[21] Van Bemmelen v. Comm'r, 155 T.C. 64, 74 (2020) *quoting* Cape Hatteras Access Pres. All. v. U.S. Dept. of Interior, 667 F. Supp. 2d 111, 114 (D.D.C. 2009).

[22] Records, like bank records, might not be available during the administrative proceedings but would be available through the use of a subpoena.

[23] Ewing v. Comm'r, 122 T.C. 32 (2004), *vacated on unrelated jurisdictional grounds*, *Ewing III*, 439 F.3d. 1009 (9th Cir. 2006).

[24] Porter v. Comm'r, 130 T.C 115 (2008). *See also* Wilson, 705 F.3d 980.

of a tax is ten years.[25] § 6015 mandates a two year statute of limitations period (as measured from the start of collections activity) to file a claim under § 6015(b) or (c). However, it was silent as to the period for filing under § 6015(f). Relying on its regulatory powers to interpret the gap in the statute, the IRS therefore imposed a two-year period of limitations for claims filed under § 6015(f).[26] The two-year limitations period, however, seriously hampered those taxpayers unable to file within the two years of collection activity and thus undercut the concept of equitable relief enshrined in § 6015(f). For example, spouses in abusive relationships might not have immediate access to mail while living with their spouse and not even know that collections activities had commenced. If they move several years later, they might only then be in a position to untangle their finances and learn about marital debts in their name. Likewise, someone facing mental or physical illness might need more time to prepare a claim. Scenarios such as these are the types of facts and circumstances that equitable relief is supposed to consider, and so such a short cap on the time to file a claim arguably went against the purpose of the statute.

The issue was first presented before the Tax Court in *Lantz v. Commissioner*,[27] where the court held that the IRS regulation was invalid because, by omitting a limitations period in subsection (f), Congress manifested an intent not to impose a deadline on equitable relief claims. The IRS appealed *Lantz* to the Seventh Circuit Court of Appeals which agreed with the IRS and reversed the Tax Court holding.[28] After the IRS won several more circuit court cases on this issue,[29] 49 members of Congress sent a letter to IRS Commissioner Shulman on April 18, 2011.[30] The letter noted that the IRS "improperly 'borrowed' the two-year statute of limitations in 6015(b) and 6015(c)" and applied it to § 6015(f). The letter further indicated that the lack of a statute of limitations was intentional, pointing to *Russello v. United States*, a Supreme Court case which held that when language included in one part of a statute is omitted in another part of the statute, it is presumed that Congress acted intentionally.[31] The letter stressed that a court may weigh all the facts and circumstances in considering appropriate

[25] I.R.C. § 6502.

[26] Treas. Reg. § 1.6015-5(b)(1) (as amended in 2002).

[27] Lantz v. Comm'r, 132 T.C. 131.

[28] Lantz v. Comm'r, 607 F.3d 479 (7th Cir. 2010).

[29] Manella v. Comm'r, 631 F.3d 115 (3rd Cir. 2011), *rev'g* 132 T.C. 196 (2009); Jones v. Comm'r, 642 F.3d 459 (4th Cir. 2011).

[30] Letter from Congressman Pete Stark, Joint Comm. on Taxation, to Douglas H. Shulman, Commissioner, I.R.S. (Apr. 18, 2011).

[31] Russello v. United States, 464 U.S. 16, 23 (1983). Taxpayers had argued the *Russello* principle in *Lantz* and other cases.

relief, and the timeframe for evaluating those facts and circumstances was not limited to a two year period.

On July 25, 2011, the IRS issued guidance that it would no longer use the two-year limitations in equitable relief cases.[32] In the future, the IRS would allow claims for the entire ten-year period in the collection statute.[33] Importantly, all cases pending on the effective date, July 25, 2011, would be subject to the longer statute. All taxpayers with claims that had been denied for untimeliness and were not litigated could reapply for relief under § 6015(f).[34]

However, the ten-year period to file a claim under § 6015(f) does not abrogate the time required to reclaim a refund off-set or other payments made to the joint liability. The time for claiming a refund based on relief from liability under § 6015(f) is still governed by the rules in I.R.C. § 6511. If a potential innocent spouse learns that their refund has been offset towards a prior joint liability, then they still just have two years from the date of the payment to use a claim for § 6015(f) relief as a refund claim for that payment. Therefore, the IRS is required to give taxpayers notice about the potential for innocent spouse claims when it offsets a refund.

V. Other Notable Early Developments

A. Nonrequesting Spouses Are Entitled to Intervene but Cannot Appeal to the Tax Court

In *King v. Commissioner*,[35] the Tax Court ruled that the nonrequesting spouse is entitled to intervene in an innocent spouse proceedings, become a party, and challenge the requesting spouse's claim for relief under § 6015(f).[36]

In *Maier v. Commissioner*,[37] the IRS granted relief under § 6015 to a requesting spouse during the administrative proceedings, eliminating the need for the requesting spouse to file a petition in the Tax Court. The nonrequesting spouse filed a petition in Tax Court seeking a redetermination of the grant of relief. Noting that it is a court of limited jurisdiction, the Tax Court held that if the requesting spouse did not file a petition for review

---

[32] I.R.S. Notice 2011-70, 2011-2 C.B. 135, *available at* http://perma.cc/LV7R-2H3U.

[33] *See* I.R.C. § 6502.

[34] Cases in which the ten-year statute had expired could not be considered for relief.

[35] King v. Comm'r, 115 T.C. 118 (2000).

[36] The IRS is required to provide the nonrequesting spouse with notice of filing of a petition claiming relief under § 6015 and to inform the nonrequesting spouse of their right to intervene. *See* Tax Ct. R. 325.

[37] Maier v. Comm'r, 119 T.C. 267 (2002), *aff'd*, 360 F.3d 361 (2d Cir. 2004).

of the IRS determination, a nonrequesting spouse could not file a petition and oppose the administrative determination granting relief.

B. *Availability of Remand*

In *Friday v. Commissioner*, in 2005, the Tax Court held that remand in standalone spousal relief cases to the IRS for further administrative development is inappropriate.[38] The Court reasoned that, because a Tax Court case brought under the standalone provision is not dependent on having a received a final determination (since it can be brought after six months of no action by the IRS), it is not a "review" of the agency determination but rather is its own separate action begun in the Court.[39]

Friday was decided in the context of fully de novo judicial review. Since the Taxpayer First Act has now restricted the Tax Court's scope of review to the administrative record, the availability of remands may be ripe for reconsideration.[40]

C. *No Jurisdiction over Second Claim for Relief*

In *Barnes v. Commissioner*,[41] the taxpayer filed a claim in 2000 seeking innocent spouse relief from tax liabilities for tax year 1997. The claim was denied. In 2007, the taxpayer filed a second claim for relief in which she provided more detailed information. The 2007 claim was also denied and the taxpayer filed a petition with the Tax Court. The IRS moved to dismiss for lack of jurisdiction. The Tax Court granted the motion, finding that the second claim was essentially duplicative of the first claim and therefore not a qualifying request for relief under Treasury Regulation § 1.6015-1(h)(5).

VI. The Taxpayer First Act of 2019

On July 1, 2019, the Taxpayer First Act came into effect. As part of this legislation, the administrative record rule was codified in § 6015(e)(7), while the standard of review was affirmed to be *de novo*. The statute states that the Tax Court's de novo review of a § 6015 relief claim must be based on the evidence available in the administrative record and other newly discovered or previously unavailable evidence. There is some emerging case law that suggests this does not bar courtroom testimony by the taxpayer or other witnesses because oral testimony is not a routine part of the administrative application process. However, the language bars a taxpayer

---

[38] Friday v. Comm'r, 124 T.C. 220 (2005).

[39] *Id.*

[40] Carlton Smith, *Should the Tax Court Allow Remands in Light of the Taxpayer First Act Innocent Spouse Provisions?*, Procedurally Taxing (Oct. 17, 2019), *available at* https://perma.cc/4YAW-8PV6.

[41] 130 T.C. 248 (2008).

from introducing documentary evidence that could have been provided at the time the administrative record was created, during the administrative application phase of the § 6015 relief claim.

The new rule applies to all innocent spouse petitions seeking innocent spouse relief in the Tax Court filed after July 1, 2019. In *Sutherland v. Commissioner*, the Tax Court clarified that the new statute could not apply to those cases where the petition was filed in the Tax Court on or before July 1, 2019. The Court pointed out that that scenario would result in a "gotcha moment" in which a taxpayer, unaware of an upcoming change in the law, did not ensure all their evidence was before the IRS before filing their petition in the Tax Court.[42] It is therefore crucial going forward that practitioners help clients develop a robust administrative record in the agency stage of innocent spouse cases.

---

[42] Sutherland v. Comm'r, 155 T.C. 95, 105 (2020).

Chapter 2: The Joint Return

I. The Joint Return Decision

Many taxpayers do not appreciate the legal effect of filing a joint return until after they receive a letter from the IRS informing them that they owe additional taxes. Whether a valid joint income tax return was filed is the threshold question in an innocent spouse analysis.

A. The Legal Consequences of a Joint Return

Tax return preparers may or may not discuss filing options with a married couple, because for most married couples the joint return is the most advantageous choice due to cost savings. The spouses have a joint return prepared, sign the return, and in most cases receive a favorable tax rate and other tax benefits. But a legal consequence of filing a joint return is joint and several liability.[1] Joint and several liability means that each spouse is individually liable for all of the tax reported on a return and for any future taxes the IRS may assess on that return, along with any related penalties and interest.

Some taxpayers believe that if they are married, they must file a joint return. However, filing a joint return is a voluntary act. Representatives should counsel their clients, especially those who are separated or going

---

[1] *See* Pullins v. Comm'r, 136 T.C. 432 (2011).

through a divorce, regarding their filing options and should ask questions to determine whether a separate return would be in the client's best interests. There are situations where filing a joint return is not worth the potential benefits, particularly in cases of domestic abuse or cases with a history of financial dishonesty between spouses. In those situations, it may be better for a client to elect Married Filing Separately status. Alternatively, if a client has been separated from their spouse for the last six months of the calendar year, and has dependents who live with them, then that client can elect to file as Head of Household, provided that they meet the other requirements of I.R.C. §§ 7703(b) and 2(b).

The following is a list of questions that should be posed to the client when evaluating the pros and cons of filing a joint return:

- Is your spouse guarded about financial information?
- Does your spouse deny you access to the family bank account?
- Does your spouse freely discuss his or her income?
- Does your spouse discourage questions about his or her income or the family's finances?
- Do you know how much income your spouse earns monthly?
- Does your spouse control the financial decisions for the family?
- Does your spouse allow you to review and ask questions about the income tax returns before you sign them?
- Does your spouse already owe tax debts to the IRS?
- Is your spouse asking you to sign a joint return that shows a balance due?
- Does your spouse owe past due child support or an educational debt?[2]
- Are there unfiled returns?
- Is your spouse mentally or physically abusive?
- Is your spouse self-employed?

If the answer to any of these questions indicates that the spouse is secretive or deceitful, the client should consider filing a separate return.

---

[2] In cases where a spouse has brought other federal debts or delinquent child support obligations into the marriage, which result in the offset of joint refunds, the other spouse may apply for "Injured Spouse Relief" using IRS Form 8379. A successful application will result in the refund being allocated so that only the portion of the refund attributable to the spouse with the pre-marital federal or child support liabilities is off-set. Joint payments already made through offset may be thus partially refunded.

B. Collection of Joint Tax Debts

The IRS is an equal opportunity debt collector. When a joint return is filed, the IRS does not look to who earned the money or who benefited from it. The IRS proceeds by identifying good collection sources and then allocating its resources to maximize collection. In cases involving low-income taxpayers, one of the most cost-effective collection methods involves offsetting the tax refund of a person who claims refundable credits.

Consider the following example. After filing a joint return, a client learns she owes taxes because her former husband, a self-employed truck driver, did not make estimated tax payments. The client, a divorced mother of two minor children, works as an employee at a bank and claims the earned income tax credit each year. Which taxpayer offers the best opportunity to collect the joint tax debt—the self-employed trucker or the wage earner? The IRS usually does not know who a self-employed taxpayer's customers are and, therefore, the IRS cannot easily levy on those sources. On the other hand, the wage earner is an easy collections target. The IRS can offset the wage earner's annual tax refunds arising from the earned income tax credit and, if necessary, can issue a levy on their wages.

II. Was a Joint Return Filed?

In any innocent spouse case, the first question is whether a joint return was in fact filed. A requesting spouse may not learn of the joint tax liability until after they receive an IRS collection notice. The spouse's first reaction may be, "I did not file a return with my spouse." Upon investigation, the spouse is told that a joint return was filed and they are liable for a deficiency or underpayment in tax. This common scenario raises the question of whether there was a valid joint return in the first place.

A. The Threshold Question for Innocent Spouse Cases

All three types of innocent spouse relief depend upon the filing of a joint return.[3] Practitioners should note that if an innocent spouse case is filed in the Tax Court, the Court's refund jurisdiction under § 6015(g) is limited to cases that meet the threshold requirements of § 6015. If there was no valid joint return, the court cannot grant a refund of payments already made by the requesting spouse on that supposed joint liability.[4]

---

[3] I.R.C. § 6015(a)(1), (b)(1), (c)(1); Raymond v. Comm'r, 119 T.C. 191 (2002).

[4] *See* James v. Comm'r, T.C. Memo 2021-7. ("Given the narrow scope of section 6015 jurisdiction, this conclusion ends the case. As we have previously observed, 'we do not have equitable powers to expand our statutorily prescribed jurisdiction no matter how unfair the circumstances may seem." [internal citation omitted.])

If a return purporting to be a joint return is filed, the IRS will generally treat the document as a joint return. Without something to alert the IRS that an issue exists regarding the joint return, the IRS is not going to investigate whether the parties intended to file a joint return. The onus is on the taxpayer who disputes filing a joint return to raise the issue and to prove that no joint return was intended.[5]

If your client maintains that they did not file a joint return, it is necessary to investigate the facts and circumstances. Reliance solely on the fact that the requesting spouse did not sign the joint return is unlikely to persuade the IRS or a court that a joint return was not intended. The IRS and the Tax Court employ the presumption of tacit consent.[6] Evidence of the facts and circumstances at the time the return was filed will be necessary to prove that there was no tacit consent.

The existence of a joint return can be challenged under various fact patterns. Some examples include:[7]

- The signature on the joint return is not the taxpayer's signature.
- The other spouse signed the taxpayer's signature to the joint return.
- The other spouse filed the joint return electronically and the document does not contain any signatures.
- The two spouses were not legally married for the entire tax year for which the return is filed.[8]
- The other spouse physically abused the taxpayer, who could not resist the other spouse's demands to sign the return. This argument is called duress and, if proved, invalidates a joint return.

In these situations it is necessary to evaluate whether the client intended to file a joint return, voluntarily signed the return, or ratified the act of the other spouse signing the return on their behalf.

B. Factors in Determining Intent

Practitioners should broadly investigate facts and circumstances that may be relevant to a determination of whether a requesting spouse intended

---

[5] Hennen v. Comm'r, 35 T.C. 747, 749 (1961).

[6] *Id.* at 747. *See* Tacit Consent Factors, I.R.M. 25.15.19.2.4.1 (10-23-2019); Heim v. Comm'r, 27 T.C. 270, 273 (1956), *aff'd* 251 F.2d 44 (8th Cir. 1958); Federbush v. Comm'r, 34 T.C. 740 (1960), *aff'd* 325 F.2d 1 (2d Cir. 1963); Shea v. Comm'r, 780 F.2d 561, 567 (6th Cir. 1986).

[7] *See* Determining if a Joint Election is Valid, I.R.M. 25.15.19.2.4.2 (10-23-2019).

[8] Generally, to file a joint return, the taxpayers must be married under state law as of the last day of the taxable year. I.R.C. §§ 6013(a), 7703(a)(1); Von Tersch v. Comm'r, 47. T.C. 415, 419 (1967). However, if a spouse dies during the tax year, then they are still considered married during the tax year provided that the other spouse did not remarry. Treas. Reg. § 301.6013-1(d).

to file a joint tax return. The Internal Revenue Manual instructs IRS employees to evaluate the following factors to determine if tacit consent was given by a taxpayer requesting innocent spouse in cases where they did not actually sign the joint return:[9]

- Whether the requesting spouse had a filing requirement. If a spouse earned enough income to trigger a filing requirement, but did not file a separate return, then that is evidence that they intended to file a joint return.
- Whether there is a history of filing joint returns in prior years.
- Whether the requesting spouse participated in preparing the joint return.
- Whether there was a tax benefit to filing jointly.
- Whether the requesting spouse signed other parts of the return, or forms following the return, or installment agreements. For example, if the requesting spouse signed a Form 4868 requesting an extension of time for the joint return or a co-signed an installment agreement that included liability on the joint return, that is evidence of an intention to file jointly.[10]
- Whether schedules include gains or losses attributable to the requesting spouse. An example would be if the joint return included a Schedule C showing income and expenses from the requesting spouse's business.
- Whether there was a legal obligation for the spouses to file a joint return. For example, a divorce agreement might stipulate that the parties will file a joint return for the final year in which they were married.

---

[9] Tacit Consent Factors, I.R.M. 25.15.19.2.4.1 (10-23-2019).

[10] The Court may look to the *Beard* test to determine whether a subsequent signed document related to the purported joint return validated the intention to file jointly. For example, in Sanchez v. Comm'r, T.C. Summ. Op. 2015-20, the Tax Court rejected the argument that a jointly signed Form 4549 ("Income Tax Discrepancy Adjustments") agreeing to changes to the return created a joint return because the form was not signed under penalties of perjury. *See also* Beard v. Comm'r, 82 T.C. 766, 777 (1984) ("The Supreme Court test to determine whether a document is sufficient for statute of limitations purposes has several elements: First, there must be sufficient data to calculate tax liability; second, the document must purport to be a return; third, there must be an honest and reasonable attempt to satisfy the requirements of the tax law; and fourth, the taxpayer must execute the return under penalties of perjury.").

C. *Suggested Questions to Determine the Existence of a Joint Return*

- Did the requesting spouse authorize the nonrequesting spouse to sign the return through their expectation that their spouse will handle financial matters?[11] This may include paying the bills, making deposits, and preparing and signing the income tax returns. A history of allowing the nonrequesting spouse to sign documents, including income tax returns, and delegating other financial matters is going to weigh heavily against a claim that the signature on the return was forged. On the other hand, the existence of physical abuse or intimidating behavior will help support a claim that the signature was not voluntary.
- Did the requesting spouse live separately from the nonrequesting spouse? In some cases, the requesting spouse lived separately from the nonrequesting spouse for part or all of the taxable year. In cases where the spouses lived apart and relations were strained, the nonrequesting spouse may have filed the joint return without the knowledge of the requesting spouse.
- Did the requesting spouse participate in the return preparation? If the requesting spouse participated in the return preparation, a claim that they did not intend to file a joint return is less compelling than if the nonrequesting spouse controlled the process and kept the requesting spouse in the dark.
- Did the requesting spouse know a return was filed? If so, when did they learn that a return had been filed? In some cases, the requesting spouse does not learn that a joint return was filed until an IRS collection notice arrives. Evidence of this would help establish that no joint return was filed.
- Did the spouses keep their financial lives separate? If the nonrequesting spouse maintained a separate bank account, did not share financial information, and controlled the family's finances, these facts help support a claim that no joint return was filed.
- Did the requesting spouse file a separate return? If the requesting spouse filed a timely separate return, then this would be strong proof that spouse did not intend to file jointly.
- Was there abusive conduct, either physical, verbal, or emotional?

---

[11] Much of this analysis may later hinge on the client's testimony as to their willingness to participate in filing a joint return and the extent to which they entrusted tax and other financial matters into their spouse's hands. *See e.g.* Soni v. Comm'r, T.C. Memo 2021-137.

III. Duress

Duress is a separate and independent ground for seeking relief, although it can be raised in an innocent spouse case. If proven, it invalidates the joint return and therefore severs the joint liability stemming from the return. If a claim was filed with the IRS's innocent spouse unit, the IRS may also grant a refund if the requesting spouse had already made payments to the joint liability in the two years preceding the application for relief. A consequence of proving duress, however, is that if the requesting spouse has brought a case under § 6015 in the Tax Court, they will not be entitled to refund relief as the Tax Court does not have jurisdiction to order a refund in cases where there was no valid joint return in the first place.[12]

In *Stanley v. Commissioner*, the Tax Court laid out two steps for proving duress. The requesting spouse must prove both that they could not resist the demand to sign the return; and that they "would not have signed the return except for the constraint applied to his or her will."[13] The Tax Court does not limit the type of constraint used to force the signing to physical violence, but rather uses a subjective standard to decide if whatever pressure was used on the requesting spouse affected their "contractual volition."[14] This is a case-by-case factual inquiry. For example, in *Stanley*, the requesting spouse convinced the Court through her testimony that she signed the return out of fear her husband would separate her from her children. Regardless of the type of constraint used, there still must be a nexus between the constraint and the signing of the return. Therefore, proving a general pattern of abuse or violence in the marriage is not enough by itself to prove duress.

IV. Options for Attacking the Joint Return

Before filing for innocent spouse relief, evaluate whether the client filed a joint return. After the necessary fact gathering is completed, the representative can reach an informed decision as to whether the client filed a joint return. Assuming that the facts point toward a conclusion that your client did not intend to file a joint return, you must carefully consider the procedural options for attacking the alleged joint return.

First, you might submit an innocent spouse request with documentation of both the primary argument (no valid joint return), and the secondary

---

[12] Successfully proving that a joint return is invalid due to duress in an innocent spouse case operates as collateral estoppel on the issue if the nonrequesting spouse intervenes in the case. *See* Hiramanek v. Comm'r, T.C. Memo 2016-92 (*Hiramanek II*) and Hiramanek v. Comm'r, T.C. Memo 2011-280 (2011) (*Hiramanek I*).

[13] Stanley v. Comm'r, 81 T.C. 634, 638 (1983).

[14] *Id. quoting* Furnish v. Comm'r, 262 F.2d 727, 733 (9th Cir 1958).

argument (innocent spouse). The I.R.M. instructs CCISO employees to first review an innocent spouse request for duress or other challenges to the return's validity, and to adjust the account if it is determined that no valid joint return was filed.[15]

This process works well if evidence is provided with the initial request and CCISO agrees that no joint return was filed. However, if the IRS does not grant relief and the requesting spouse appeals to the Tax Court, the requesting spouse will be limited to arguments regarding innocent spouse relief, as the Tax Court in a standalone 6015(e) case cannot provide relief if there was no valid joint return.[16]

Other avenues for contesting an invalid joint return outside of the innocent spouse process may include:

- Filing a Married Filing Separately tax return;
- Offer in compromise based on doubt as to liability;
- Audit reconsideration;
- Paying the tax in full and filing a refund claim, then filing a refund suit.[17]

V. Should You Argue There Was No Joint Return?

If the facts are unclear as to whether a joint return was intended, it still may not be in your client's best interests to claim there was no joint return. There are two common scenarios in which arguing against the validity of the return may have adverse results.

First, if the requesting spouse otherwise had a filing obligation, then arguing there was no joint return may result in substantial liability if they made enough income independently to trigger a filing requirement. They could find themselves with significant deficiencies and non-filing penalties of their own.

---

[15] *See* Return Signed Under Duress, I.R.M. 25.15.1.2.3 (06-26-2017) and Forged Signatures, I.R.M. 25.15.1.2.4 (06-26-2017). Form 8857 requires the taxpayer to answer whether or not a joint return was filed. If the answer is "no," then the form instructions direct the taxpayer not to complete the Form 8857. Nevertheless, if the taxpayer believes that the return is not a joint return, they should state that no joint return was filed but argue in the alternative that if the return is determined to be a joint return, then they are entitled to innocent spouse relief. If the IRS determines that no joint return was filed, the taxpayer effectively avoids the tax attributable to their spouse's income items.

[16] Abdelhadi v. Comm'r, T.C. Memo. 2018-183.

[17] The IRS not view spousal forgery as identity theft; thus, filing an identity theft affidavit will not obtain review of an invalid joint return. *See* Invalid Joint Election Consideration, I.R.M. 25.23.4.8.1.4.1. (10-01-2020); *see also* Forgery, I.R.M. 25.15.19.2.5 (10-23-2019).

Second, if the requesting spouse seeks a refund of payments made towards the joint liability, and if they bring the case as a standalone claim into the Tax Court, then the Court will have no jurisdiction to order such a refund.

An example of the first scenario occurred in the 2017 case *Okorogu v. Commissioner*.[18] In *Okorogu*, a woman raised innocent spouse relief as a deficiency defense in the Tax Court. She alleged severe physical, sexual, and emotional abuse during her marriage. She was particularly vulnerable in that she had immigrated to the United States from Nigeria and was unfamiliar with the United States tax system. Her husband, an engineer in California, completely controlled the family finances as well as her personal access to money. She could not even shop for clothing without his permission.

In a surprise twist, it was the husband who tried to argue that there was no valid joint return. He contended that he had forged his wife's signature and filed two joint returns without her consent. He even alleged that *he* did not really intend the returns to be joint. The husband's motive was not altruistic. He was seeking to have the wife denied innocent spouse relief because the IRS had conceded that she would be entitled to relief if the returns were valid. It mattered because the wife, who had worked as a lab researcher, had made enough money to trigger filing requirements on her own during the years at issue. If the joint returns were invalid, then she was out of filing compliance.

The Court decided the returns were valid under the tacit consent doctrine. Specifically, it looked at the marital history in which the husband always controlled the family finances and prepared and filed all the joint returns. It also looked to the tax rate benefit that came with the joint filing and further gave credence to the wife's testimony that she would have consented to having the returns filed jointly had she known she had a filing obligation and had he presented the prepared returns for her signature. The Court therefore determined that the returns were valid and that she was entitled to innocent spouse relief.

The inability to obtain refund relief without a valid joint return appeared in the 2021 case *James v. Commissioner*.[19] In *James*, an ex-wife filed for innocent spouse relief after her 2014 and 2016 refunds from single returns she filed post-divorce were taken to pay towards liability from a 2010 joint return with her ex-husband. The problem with her innocent spouse request, however, was that the couple had been divorced since 2006.

At the agency level, the IRS had found she was ineligible for innocent spouse relief because there was no valid joint return for 2010. However,

---

[18] Okorogu v. Comm'r, T.C. Memo 2017-53.

[19] James v. Comm'r, T.C. Memo 2021-7.

it did refund her 2016 payment toward the liability. The agency did not grant a refund for her 2014 payment because it was time barred under the two-year limits of I.R.C. § 6511(a), and so the ex-wife brought her case into the Tax Court.

The Tax Court did not reach the merits of her § 6511(a) argument because it denied her innocent spouse relief under § 6015 for lack of a joint return. The Court emphasized that its jurisdiction to decide cases under § 6015 is narrow in scope and that it does not have any equitable power to expand that jurisdiction, even in the face of unfair results.

VI. Protecting the Refund Statute

To protect your client's access to a refund when arguing there was no joint return, it may be necessary to file a protective claim by submitting a new Form 1040 return in which the taxpayer elects married filing separately status.[20] It is also wise to file the protective claim as soon as possible after you decide to argue that no joint return was filed because the amount of a refund is limited by section 6511(b)(2). Refunds are limited to payments made within two years of the date the administrative claim for refund is filed.[21] If you wait until the court rules on the issue in a standalone proceeding, the time limits for filing a refund claim under section 6511(b)(2) may have expired on some of the payments. By filing a protective claim, you protect your client's interests in the refund.

---

[20] A protective claim is very useful. It informs the IRS that if your primary position is not accepted by the IRS or the Tax Court, then the position in your protective claim is activated. An important reason for filing the protective claim is to file a timely claim for refund.

[21] I.R.C. § 6511(b)(2)(B).

Chapter 3: Section 6015

I. Three Types of Innocent Spouse Relief

A. Section 6015(b)

Section 6015(b) provides relief where:

- A joint return was filed;
- On the return there is an understatement of tax attributable to erroneous items of the nonrequesting spouse;
- In signing the return, the requesting spouse did not know, or have reason to know, that there was such understatement; and
- Considering all the facts and circumstances, it is inequitable to hold the requesting spouse liable for the deficiency in tax.

B. Section 6015(c)

Section 6015(c) allows a requesting spouse who has left the relationship to elect relief from a portion of the understatement attributable to the nonrequesting spouse, if certain conditions are met.

An individual is eligible to elect relief under § 6015(c) if:

- At the time the election is filed, the requesting spouse is widowed, or is no longer married to, or is legally separated from the nonrequesting spouse;[1] or
- The requesting spouse was not a member of the same household as the nonrequesting spouse at any time during the 12 month period ending on the date the election is filed.

The requesting spouse has the burden of proof with respect to the portion of the deficiency allocable to their income.[2] The IRS can deny relief under subsection (c) if it can demonstrate that the requesting spouse had actual knowledge of the income item, but the IRS has the burden of proof on this issue.[3]

C. Section 6015(f)

Section 6015(f) provides the Secretary with discretion to grant equitable relief from either an understatement or an underpayment of tax. A condition of relief under § 6015(f) is that relief is not allowable under either § 6015(b) or (c).[4] Thus, regardless of how a claim is styled, the IRS is required to first consider eligibility for relief under § 6015(b) and (c). Equitable relief is the only type of relief available for underpayment cases; that is, where the return shows the correct amount of tax but the liability is unpaid.

D. First Collection Activity: The Two-Year Rule for 6015(b) and (c) Claims

Claims under I.R.C. §§ 6015(b) and (c) must be made within two years of the first IRS collection activity for the debt. The Treasury regulation defines collection activity as any of the following:[5]

- Notice of intent to levy and right to a Collection Due Process ("CDP") hearing under I.R.C. § 6330;
- A refund offset under I.R.C. § 6402;
- The filing of a collection suit by the United States; or
- The filing of a claim by the United States in a court proceeding "in which the requesting spouse is a party or which involves property of the requesting spouse."

---

[1] Treas. Reg. § 1.6015-3(a) (as amended in 2002).
[2] I.R.C. § 6015(c)(2).
[3] I.R.C. § 6015(c)(3)(C).
[4] I.R.C. § 6015(f)(1)(b). *See also infra* Chapter 6, II (*Revenue Procedure 2013-34—Guidelines for Equitable Relief*).
[5] Treas. Reg. § 1.6015-5(b)(2)(i).

The regulation clarifies that "collection activity" for § 6015 purposes does *not* include:

- The filing of a notice of federal tax lien;
- A notice of deficiency; or
- A demand for payment of tax.

Note that CDP rights under I.R.C. § 6320 (triggered by the filing of a notice of federal tax lien) look very similar to CDP levy notices under I.R.C. § 6330, but do not start the two-year period running.

E. Types of Liabilities Eligible for Section 6015 Relief

Section 6015 applies to tax liabilities stemming from a joint federal income tax return. When relief is granted for a certain tax liability, the taxpayer is also relieved of liability for the interest and penalties associated with the liability.[6] This much is clear. However, at least two situations have arisen in which the taxpayer and the government disagree on whether spousal relief is available.

First, may a taxpayer request innocent spouse relief only for penalties[7] and interest? The IRS often takes the position that equitable relief can only be considered if there is a deficiency or an underpayment of tax. The Tax Court has rejected this position several times, most recently in 2016.[8] However, the IRS continues to advocate for a narrow reading of § 6015, and it may seek to distinguish or minimize the court's precedents.[9] Practitioners should be prepared to advocate for judicial review in such cases.

Second, is spousal relief available for erroneous refund liabilities?[10] The IRS takes the position that an erroneous refund liability is not a "tax" or a

---

[6] Washington v. Comm'r, 120 T.C. 137 (2003).

[7] We use the term "penalties" colloquially, encompassing both items labeled in the Code as penalties, such as the accuracy penalty under I.R.C. § 6662, and those labeled as "additions to tax," such as the late filing penalty under I.R.C. § 6651(a)(1).

[8] Boyle v. Comm'r, T.C. Memo. 2016-87 (taxpayer sought relief from interest and additions to tax; tax liability remained unpaid at time of trial); Kollar v. Comm'r, 131 T.C. 191, 196–197 (2008) (taxpayer sought relief from interest after having paid the tax due).

[9] *See, e.g.*, emailed Chief Counsel Advice No. 202141006, ID CCA_2020011709541644 (Jan. 17, 2020; released Oct. 15, 2021), reprinted at 2021 TNTF 199-35 (Oct. 18, 2021). In this non-precedential email, the IRS concludes that assessed penalties and interest cannot be considered for spousal relief if there is no deficiency or underpayment. The CCA distinguishes *Boyle* on the grounds that Mr. Boyle's tax liability remained unpaid at the time of trial, although he was only seeking relief from interest and penalties. However, the CCA fails to distinguish *Kollar*, and its position is inconsistent with that precedent.

[10] For background on erroneous refund liabilities, *see* IRS Office of Chief Counsel, Significant Service Center Advice Memorandum No. 200014033 (Apr. 7, 2000), https://perma.cc/7ELX-6B73.

"deficiency" and therefore § 6015 does not apply.[11] In litigating this issue, practitioners should be alert to the distinction between a rebate refund (caused by an IRS determination of tax liability), and a nonrebate refund (unconnected to the substance of a tax liability; for example, a duplicate refund check).[12] It would seem that a stronger case might be made for rebate refunds to be characterized as tax liabilities within the meaning of § 6015(f).

II. Duty of Inquiry

When a taxpayer seeking spousal relief signs a return without reading it, the case may present a difficult issue. A court may find that the failure to review the return, often referred to in the cases as "turning a blind eye," results in constructive knowledge.[13] Cases hold that spousal relief provisions are intended to protect the innocent, not the intentionally ignorant.[14] Representing a client who did not review the return requires an understanding of a taxpayer's "duty of inquiry" and how it affects your client's case. A finding of constructive knowledge can result in your client losing both the knowledge element under § 6015(b) and the knowledge factor under § 6015(f).

A. Discussion

Each taxpayer has a duty to correctly report and pay his or her tax liabilities. A taxpayer cannot simply delegate the duty to file and pay taxes to his or her spouse and then claim innocent spouse relief.[15]

In both omitted income and erroneous deduction cases, a taxpayer who signs a return without reviewing it may be considered to have constructive knowledge of the understatement for failing to inquire into the contents of the return.[16] For example, in Hayman v. Commissioner the requesting spouse wrote checks, signed multiple documents pertaining to a partnership with the nonrequesting spouse, was given extensive memos detailing

---

[11] *See* Respondent's *Memorandum of Law in Support of Respondent's Motion to Dismiss for Lack of Jurisdiction* in LaRosa v. Comm'r, U.S. Tax Court Docket No. 10164-20 (Nov. 10, 2020). Ms. LaRosa's liability stemmed from an erroneous refund of overpayment interest. As of this writing, the Tax Court has not ruled on the government's motion to dismiss.

[12] *See* O'Bryant v. United States, 49 F.3d 340, 342 (7th Cir. 1995).

[13] Price v. Comm'r, 887 F.2d 959, 965 (9th Cir. 1989) (summarizing case law).

[14] *See, e.g.*, Cohen v. Comm'r, T.C. Memo. 1987-537 (denying relief where requesting spouse had signed the joint return without questioning and "should have taken the time or effort to inquire;" the Court found that her "ostrich imitation" was not reasonable). *Cohen* addresses prior § 6013(e), which offered similar relief to § 6015(b).

[15] Hayman v. Comm'r, 992 F.2d 1256, 1262 (2d Cir. 1993), *aff'g* T.C. Memo. 1992-228; Pullins v. Comm'r, 136 T.C. 432 (2011). *See also Price*, 887 F.2d at 965; Butler v. Comm'r, 114 T.C. 276, 284 (2000).

[16] *Hayman*, 992 F.2d at 1262.

the tax shelter investments, and had a history of dealing with the family's financial matters. Even though she claimed to have signed documents without understanding them, the court found that the requesting spouse had reason to know of the understatement and denied her claim under prior § 6013(e).[17]

In underpayment cases, a taxpayer who failed to review the return may be considered to have constructive knowledge of the tax liability, which can present challenges for proving a reasonable belief that the nonrequesting spouse would pay the debt.[18] In *Pullins v. Commissioner* the requesting spouse signed returns without reviewing them, and the Court found she had constructive knowledge of the taxes reported on the returns. The Court then evaluated whether Ms. Pullins had reason to know that the nonrequesting spouse would not pay those liabilities. Ms. Pullins lost the knowledge factor but still won equitable relief under § 6015(f).[19]

Regardless of the subsection under which relief is sought, the courts employ a subjective test. The question is whether a reasonably prudent person, under the circumstances the requesting spouse faced at the time the return was signed, could be expected to know that the tax liability was erroneous (in an understatement case), or that the liability would not be paid (in an underpayment case), or that further investigation was warranted.[20] Would a reasonably prudent taxpayer in the requesting spouse's position have questioned the erroneous item?[21] Would they have questioned whether the liability would be paid? If there are sufficient facts to put the requesting spouse on notice as to the possibility of an understatement or underpayment, the requesting spouse has a duty to inquire about the matter.

In applying the subjective test to a given taxpayer, courts will consider the following issues, known as the *Price* factors:

- the taxpayer's level of education;
- the taxpayer's involvement in the family's business and financial affairs;
- unusual or lavish expenditures inconsistent with the couple's level of income or standard of living; and

---

[17] *Id.*

[18] *See* Briley v. Comm'r, T.C. Memo. 2019-55; *see also infra* Chapter 6, II (*Revenue Procedure 2003-61—Guidelines for Equitable Relief*).

[19] *Pullins*, 136 T.C. at 443–45, 449–50, 455.

[20] *See* Juell v. Comm'r, T.C. Memo. 2007-219 at *3–4. Granting relief under § 6015(b), the Court in *Juell* found that the requesting spouse had satisfied her duty of inquiry where she questioned the nonrequesting spouse, and he repeatedly assured her of the accuracy of their joint returns.

[21] Price v. Comm'r, 887 F.2d 959 (9th Cir. 1989).

- the evasiveness or deceit of the taxpayer's spouse as to the couple's finances.[22]

The duty of inquiry can be satisfied if the requesting spouse questions the nonrequesting spouse about the return and the nonrequesting spouse assures her that it is correct or that he will pay the liability.[23]

B. Meeting the Duty of Inquiry

Many clients first fill out the Request for Innocent Spouse Relief (Form 8857) by themselves and truthfully indicate that they did not review the returns.[24] The problem is that they often do not adequately describe the circumstances at the time the return was signed, which often explain or mitigate their failure to review the return. Here are some examples: 1) the nonrequesting spouse did not tolerate questions or disagreement; 2) the requesting spouse believed that the nonrequesting spouse would retaliate if questions were asked; or 3) the nonrequesting spouse demanded that the requesting spouse sign the return as prepared and did not permit any kind of review.[25]

When a taxpayer indicates on the Form 8857 that they did not review the return and the IRS charges them with constructive knowledge, the representative should gather any available facts that establish that the requesting spouse could not reasonably review the return or ask questions due to a history of threats and violence or the possibility of retaliation. Or, perhaps the requesting spouse took steps sufficient to satisfy the duty

---

[22] *Id.* at 965. The "Price factors" are still widely used today even though the case predates today's § 6015. *See, e.g.*, Jacobsen v. Comm'r, T.C. Memo. 2018-115, *aff'd*, 950 F.3d 414 (7th Cir. 2020) (noting that the *Price* factors largely overlap with the § 6015(b)(1)(C) factors in Regulation § 1.6015-2(c)). In *Jacobsen*, the Tax Court granted Mr. Jacobsen relief for tax year 2010 under § 6015(b), finding that he had no reason to know of his wife's embezzlement income when that return was filed. Conversely the Court denied relief for 2011 under all subsections, placing overwhelming weight on Mr. Jacobsen's actual knowledge as of the date the 2011 return was filed.

[23] *See Juell, supra* n. 20. and cases cited therein. *See also* Crouse v. Comm'r , T.C. Memo. 2011-97. The *Crouse* case hinged on whether the requesting spouse, who did not review the return, met her duty of inquiry. The IRS argued for charging her with constructive notice of the funds embezzled by the nonrequesting spouse. Under § 6015(b), the Court held that a reasonably prudent person in her circumstances could not be expected to know of the omitted income. Although the taxpayer did not ask questions, the Court found that the nonrequesting spouse would have reassured her that the return was accurate, so the inquiry would have been futile. *But see* John E. Rogers and Frances L. Rogers, et al. v. Comm'r, T.C. Memo. 2020-91 at *7 (requesting spouse's "blind confidence in her husband" and "emotional decision to ignore the facts and circumstances she well knew on an intellectual level is not a lack of knowledge for purposes of § 6015(b) … and (f).").

[24] On Form 8857, if a taxpayer confirms that they did not review the returns before the returns were signed, the form instructs the taxpayer to explain why they did not review the return.

[25] In some cases, the nonrequesting spouse simply files the return electronically without allowing the requesting spouse to see it. In other cases, the nonrequesting spouse goes alone to the tax preparer and later demands that the requesting spouse sign the prepared return or e-file authorization.

of inquiry.[26] If the IRS resists the client's explanation and denies relief, the only option may be to file a petition in the Tax Court for a review of the adverse determination. If the case proceeds to trial, the outcome will depend to a great extent on the requesting spouse's credibility.

C. Duty of Inquiry and Actual Knowledge

Because the IRS must prove actual knowledge, a failure to review the return would not automatically cause the loss of the knowledge element in a § 6015(c) case. A showing of constructive knowledge does not meet the IRS's burden to prove actual knowledge.[27] However, the IRS will oppose relief if the requesting spouse made a deliberate effort to avoid learning about the erroneous item.[28]

III. Timing Considerations and Successive Claims for Relief

Even though the three types of spousal relief have different criteria, the IRS's practice is to consider all three whenever a taxpayer requests relief.[29] For example, if a taxpayer asks for consideration of § 6015(c) relief and the IRS denies relief under that subsection, the IRS will then consider whether traditional relief or equitable relief is available even though the taxpayer has not requested those forms of relief. Because the facts and circumstances relevant to relief often change dramatically over time, it is important to understand the limitations applicable to successive spousal relief claims to advise your client on the best timing for a relief claim.

The most important limitations are those on judicial review. If the IRS denies spousal relief the taxpayer may appeal the denial administratively with the IRS. In some cases, the taxpayer may also appeal to the U.S. Tax Court. Later chapters describe these procedures in more detail.

A. Reconsideration

The IRS will reconsider claims for innocent spouse relief in a process akin to the audit reconsideration program.[30] Successful reconsideration requires that a taxpayer submit additional information that was not considered in the first request.[31]

---

[26] *See, e.g.*, Price, 887 F.2d at 966.

[27] *See* Culver v. Comm'r, 116 T.C. 189; Richard v. Comm'r, T.C. Memo. 2011-144; Bishop v. Comm'r, 2018 T.C. Sum. Op. 1.

[28] Treas. Reg. § 1.6015-3(c)(2)(iv).

[29] *See* Treas. Reg. § 1.6015-1(a)(2) (as amended in 2002). IRS Form 8857 does not have a place on which to indicate the subsection under which the taxpayer seeks relief; rather, the form is designed to function as a single request for all forms of spousal relief.

[30] *See* Reconsiderations, I.R.M. 25.15.17 (03-05-2019).

[31] Terms, I.R.M. 25.15.17.1.4 (03-05-2019).

The innocent spouse reconsideration program, like the audit reconsideration program, is a matter of administrative grace. The IRS is not required by I.R.C. § 6015 to reconsider denials of innocent spouse relief.[32]

Importantly, a determination made on reconsideration is not generally issued as a final determination under § 6015(e). So, while taxpayers have the right to an Appeals conference if reconsideration results in denial, there is no statutory right to file a petition in Tax Court seeking review of the redetermination decision.

In limited circumstances, the IRS may issue a second final determination letter.[33] The regulations allow for a second "final determination" under § 6015(c), if marital status has changed.[34] The I.R.M. also allows a second final determination letter in cases of delay or error on the part of the IRS, and in cases of taxpayer fraud.[35] If the IRS mistakenly issues a second final determination letter, the Tax Court will have jurisdiction over a timely appeal.[36]

B. Don't Ask (the Court) Twice

The doctrine of res judicata prevents re-litigation of disputes, including tax disputes.[37] Litigants cannot later bring to court any claim that could have been litigated in the first case. Since spousal relief is an affirmative defense to a deficiency, this doctrine would foreclose a Tax Court appeal under I.R.C. § 6015(e) if there had previously been a petition for redetermination of a deficiency for the tax year at issue.[38]

I.R.C. § 6015(g)(2) offers limited relief from this harsh result. A prior court decision involving the tax year at issue is not res judicata if spousal relief was not an issue in the proceeding, and the requesting spouse did not participate meaningfully in the court proceeding.[39] Both conditions must be met. It is generally simple to tell whether spousal relief was at

---

[32] Prior to March 2008, the IRS resisted any reconsideration. *See* National Taxpayer Advocate 2006 Annual Report to Congress Vol. I § 2, at 537 (2007), *available at* http://perma.cc/DA5R-77RM.

[33] Reg. § 1.6015-5(c)(1).

[34] *See* Reg. §§ 1.6015-1(h)(5), 1.6015-5(c)(1), 1.6015-3.

[35] Issuing Second Preliminary and Final Determinations for the Same Relief Request, I.R.M. 25.15.17.7 (03-05-2019).

[36] *See* Vera v. Comm'r, 157 T. C. 78 (2021).

[37] Koprowski v. Comm'r, 138 T.C. 54, 60 (2012) (*citing* Comm'r v. Sunnen, 333 U.S. 591, 597-598 (1948)).

[38] *See id.* at 62-63 (noting the four conditions for res judicata and applying them to a deficiency case).

[39] *Id.* at 65; I.R.C. § 6015(g)(2). If a spouse meaningfully participated, then they could have raised § 6015 in the prior case. *See* Treas. Reg. § 1.6015-1(e).

issue in a prior case.[40] Meaningful participation is fact-specific, though it requires more than merely signing the petition.[41] Signing and reviewing documents, participating in settlement discussions, and testifying at trial may indicate meaningful participation.

In *Deihl v. Commissioner*,[42] the taxpayer and her husband filed deficiency petitions covering the tax years 1996, 1997, and 1998. The pleadings raised the issue of innocent spouse relief for 1996, but not for the other years. The petitions were signed by counsel hired by Mr. Diehl. Though spousal relief was raised in one petition, the issue was not tried. Mrs. Diehl testified briefly at trial but did not review any documents, participate in any case-related meetings or settlement negotiations, or even meet her counsel prior to trial. During the litigation, the taxpayer and her spouse were living together and thus she was not eligible to elect § 6015(c) relief. The Tax Court ultimately determined deficiencies for all three tax years. Shortly thereafter the taxpayer's husband died and the taxpayer filed a claim for innocent spouse relief. The IRS denied the claim and the taxpayer filed a petition for judicial review.

The Tax Court held that the taxpayer did not materially participate in the deficiency proceedings, and while she had raised innocent spouse relief for 1996 in the petition, she had not raised spousal relief for 1997 or 1998 and it was not addressed in the litigation. Accordingly, the court held the following: 1) the court could decide the taxpayer's request for innocent spouse relief under all three subsections for 1997 and 1998; and 2) because she was not eligible to claim innocent spouse relief under § 6015(c) for 1996 at the time of the deficiency proceedings, she could still raise a claim for 1996 under § 6015(c) in the stand-alone proceeding.

C. *Timing Considerations*

Based on the foregoing, a representative should consider the following issues before they file a claim for spousal relief:

- Has the IRS initiated collection activity? If the IRS has taken a collection action that begins the two-year period of limitations for claims under § 6015(b) and (c), when does the deadline run?
- If the period of limitations is still open, does the taxpayer have a strong case for relief under either § 6015(b) or (c)? If the case is

---

[40] Any spousal relief claim may put all available spousal relief claims at issue. *See* Thurner v. Comm'r, 121 T.C. 43 (2003), *aff'd*, 255 Fed. Appx. 90 (7th Cir. 2007) (finding equitable relief claims to be "subordinate and ancillary" to claims for relief under I.R.C. § 6015(b) or (c)).

[41] Diehl v. Comm'r, 134 T.C. 156 (2010) (discussing cases addressing the meaningful participation standard).

[42] *Id.*

strong, then it may be a good decision to file the election as early as possible.[43]

- Is the case under I.R.C. § 6015(b) and (c) weak? If the case is weak, it is necessary to consider the strength of the case under § 6015(f). If the taxpayer cannot prove a majority of the equitable relief factors, then it may be a good decision to wait to request relief until more circumstances favor the requesting spouse.[44]
- If the client has a pending deficiency case in the Tax Court, the taxpayer may have no choice but to assert their spousal relief claim as an affirmative defense. The failure to raise the affirmative defense may result in the taxpayer being barred from litigating a later claim.

---

[43] If the couple is going through a divorce or has not been living apart for 12 months, filing the claim prior to these changes in marital status may be advantageous. This is because the one occasion where the regulations allow a second claim is when the marital status changes. *See* Treas. Reg. § 1.6015-1(h)(5).

[44] If the knowledge factor is negative, it is particularly important that the requesting spouse have many positive factors on their side. *See infra* Chapter 6, II.D.3 (*Knowledge or Reason to Know*).

Chapter 4: Section 6015(b)

I. The Elements of I.R.C. Section 6015(b)

Section 6015(b)(1) provides relief where:

- A joint return was filed;
- On the return there is an understatement of tax attributable to erroneous items of the nonrequesting spouse;
- In signing the return, the requesting spouse did not know, or have reason to know, that there was such understatement;
- Considering all the facts and circumstances, it is inequitable to hold the requesting spouse liable for the deficiency in tax; and
- The taxpayer seeks relief no later than two years after the date the IRS begins collection activity.

The requirements of § 6015(b)(1) are stated in the conjunctive. Therefore, each condition must be satisfied.

A. Discussion

Section 6015(b), known as "traditional relief," is similar to § 6013(e), which provided spousal relief prior to the 1998 amendments.[1] Section

[1] I.R.S. Restructuring and Reform Act of 1998, Pub. L. No. 105-206, tit. IV, § 3201, 112 Stat. 685, 740 (repealing § 6013(e)).

6015(b) relates only to deficiencies, not underpayments of tax. There are some differences between § 6015(b) and former § 6013(e), such as the proportionate relief allowed by § 6015(b)(2), but in deciding cases under § 6015(b), courts will consider cases interpreting § 6013(e) as instructive.[2]

The I.R.M. suggests that examiners consider attribution before reviewing any other factor.[3] Attribution is the ownership of or responsibility for the specific items that caused the understatement of tax (such as unreported income, inflated deductions, or excess credits). Items attributable to the requesting spouse will not qualify for relief under § 6015(b).[4]

As with all spousal relief claims, knowledge is a crucial factor. The knowledge requirement under § 6015(b) relates to knowledge of the transaction or item of omitted income, not whether the taxpayer knew of the tax consequences of the transaction.[5] The court will consider whether a reasonably prudent person in the requesting spouse's shoes would have had reason to know of the understatement, or would have had reason to question the accuracy of the return.[6]

In determining whether it would be inequitable to hold the requesting spouse liable, all of the facts and circumstances of the case will be considered.[7] The applicable regulation incorporates by reference the IRS's guidance on equitable relief under § 6015(f).[8] Thus, the equitable factors considered under § 6015(b) are the same factors considered under § 6015(f).[9] Nevertheless, the courts often make two primary inquiries: 1) whether the requesting spouse received a significant benefit; and 2) whether the nonrequesting spouse's conduct included concealing, overreaching or wrongdoing.[10] Use of funds for normal support will not be considered a significant benefit.[11]

---

[2] Butler v. Comm'r, 114 T.C. 276 (2000); Jonson v. Comm'r, 118 T.C. 106 (2002); Briley v. Comm'r, T.C. Memo. 2019-55.

[3] *See* Understatement Attributable to Erroneous Item of NRS, I.R.M. 25.15.3.7.2 (12-12-2016).

[4] The I.R.M. goes into considerable detail on how to allocate the understatement in specific situations. *See* Allocating a Deficiency, I.R.M. 25.15.3.8.3 (12-12-2016). For further discussion of attribution issues, *see infra* Chapter 6, II.A.2 (*Attributing the Liability*).

[5] Cheshire v. Comm'r, 115 T.C. 183, 192 (2000), *aff'd*, 282 F.3d 326 (5th Cir. 2002).

[6] *See supra* Chapter 3, II (*Duty of Inquiry*). If there were reasons to suspect an understatement but the requesting spouse was afraid to ask questions because of abusive treatment, the court may find the knowledge requirement satisfied. *See* Kistner v. Comm'r, 18 F.3d 1521 (11th Cir. 1994).

[7] Treas. Reg. § 6015-2(d).

[8] *Id.*

[9] Alt v. Comm'r, 119 T.C. 306, 316 (2002), *aff'd*, 101 Fed. App'x 34 (6th Cir. 2004); Hall v. Comm'r, T.C. Memo 2014-171; Bartak v. Comm'r, T.C. Memo 2004-83. For a discussion of the Commissioner's equitable relief guidance, *see infra* Chapter 6, II (*Revenue Procedure 2013-34—Guidelines for Equitable Relief*).

[10] Alt v. Comm'r, 119 T.C. at 314.

[11] Treas. Reg. § 6015-2(d); Flynn v. Comm'r, 93 T.C. 355, 367 (1989).

Under § 6015(b), the burden of proof is on the taxpayer to prove they are entitled to relief.[12] A spouse who is granted relief under § 6015(b) can recover refunds of amounts that they paid, subject to the time limitations of § 6511.[13]

II. Refundable Credits and Substantial Benefit

In some cases, the IRS may disallow a claim for relief under § 6015(b) for the sole reason that the requesting spouse received a refund due to the earned income credit or child tax credit. The IRS may contend that if the requesting spouse received a portion of the refund, they received a substantial benefit and therefore it is not inequitable to hold the requesting spouse liable for the deficiency. While there are few decided cases on this point, the Tax Court disagreed with the IRS in *Ybarra v. Commissioner*.[14]

Ybarra presented a classic fact pattern. The taxpayer and her husband reported $27,201 in adjusted gross income. They claimed three exemptions for their children, the child tax credit ($1,916), and the earned income tax credit ($1,734), resulting in a refund of $3,753. The return failed to include three income items, totaling about $3,900, all attributable to the nonrequesting spouse. The recalculated tax reduced the credits and resulted in a deficiency of $771.

The taxpayer filed a claim for innocent spouse relief under § 6015 and the respondent issued a final determination letter denying relief. In its trial memorandum, the IRS conceded that it did not have any evidence that the taxpayer knew or had reason to know about her husband's omitted income. The only issue presented for trial was whether, under § 6015(b), it was inequitable to hold the taxpayer liable for the deficiency.

In deciding whether it was inequitable to hold the taxpayer liable, the Tax Court considered two factors: 1) whether there had been a significant benefit to the requesting spouse; and 2) whether there was concealment, wrongdoing, or overreaching on the part of the nonrequesting spouse. The IRS apparently argued that to the extent that the taxpayer received a portion of the refund, it would not be inequitable to hold her liable. But that argument did not carry the day.

The Tax Court noted that the taxpayer had monthly wages of $1,600, other assistance of $250 a month, and the taxpayer's husband did not provide any household or child support. The taxpayer used the refund for basic living expenses, and the IRS conceded that the funds involved did not provide a significant benefit beyond normal support. The proof

---

[12] *See* Tax Ct. R. 142(a); *see also* Alt, 119 T.C. at 311; *infra* Chapter 12, I (*Burden of Proof*).

[13] *See infra* Chapter 13 (*Obtaining a Refund from the IRS*).

[14] T.C. Summ. Op. 2008-2.

showed that the taxpayer did not make any extravagant purchases and lived a modest life. In addition to the foregoing, the Tax Court found that the taxpayer's husband concealed the unreported income from her. The Tax Court ruled that the requesting spouse was entitled to relief under § 6015.

Chapter 5: Section 6015(c)

I. The Elements of Section 6015(c)

A person may elect separation of liability under § 6015(c) if:

- A joint return was filed;
- On the return there is an understatement of tax attributable at least partly to erroneous items of the nonrequesting spouse;
- At the time the election is made, the requesting spouse is no longer married to or is legally separated from the nonrequesting spouse, or has not been a member of the same household as the nonrequesting spouse for at least 12 months;[1] and
- The election is made within two years of the first collection activity.[2]

But, several wrinkles may complicate the availability of relief:

- Relief is not available if the IRS demonstrates that the requesting spouse had actual knowledge of an item contributing to the deficiency, unless the return was signed under duress;[3]

---

[1] I.R.C. § 6015(c)(3)(A)(i). *See* Vetrano v. Comm'r, 116 T.C. 272, 283 (2001).
[2] I.R.C. § 6015(c)(3)(B).
[3] I.R.C. § 6015(c)(3)(C).

- The election is invalid if assets were transferred between the spouses as part of a fraudulent scheme;[4]
- The requesting spouse's separate liability must be increased by the value of any asset that was transferred to them by the nonrequesting spouse for the principal purpose of avoiding tax or payment of tax;[5] and
- In the liability allocation, the requesting spouse will be allocated items of the nonrequesting spouse to the extent they gave rise to a tax benefit enjoyed by the requesting spouse on the joint return.[6]

If the requesting spouse is granted relief under § 6015(c), § 6015(g)(3) bars a refund. Refunds are only available under subsections (b) and (f). Thus, obtaining a refund through an innocent spouse claim requires good planning.[7]

A. Discussion

Separation of liability is an independent ground for spousal relief, created in 1998. In general, an item giving rise to a deficiency is allocated between the spouses as though they had filed separate returns.[8] In cases of fraud, the IRS has discretion to allocate items differently.[9]

Unlike § 6015(b), the requesting spouse does not have to prove that it would be inequitable to hold them liable. On the other hand, if the deficiency involved the disallowance of deductions, your client might not be entitled to full relief even though the deductions are entirely attributable to the nonrequesting spouse. If your client benefited from the deductions, § 6015(d)(3)(B) may preclude relief.[10]

---

[4] I.R.C. § 6015(c)(3)(A)(ii).

[5] I.R.C. § 6015(c)(4).

[6] I.R.C. § 6015(d)(3)(B).

[7] Before the IRS will consider relief under § 6015(f), it will review whether relief is available under subsection (b) or (c). *See* I.R.C. § 6015(f)(1)(B). Also, in cases claiming relief under subsection (b), the IRS may seek to grant relief under subsection (c) and thereby deny any refunds. The IRS takes the position that all subsections will be considered when an individual requests spousal relief. Full and Objective Consideration of All Relief Provisions, I.R.M. 25.15.6.9(3) (06-19-2017); *see also* Treas. Reg. § 1.6015-1(a)(2).

[8] I.R.C. § 6015(d)(3)(A). The regulation sets out the IRS's approach to allocating items of income, deductions, credits, taxes other than income tax and the alternative minimum tax, and additions to tax. Treas. Reg. § 1.6015-3(d)(2).

[9] I.R.C. § 6015(d)(3)(C); Treas. Reg. § 1.6015-3(d)(2)(ii).

[10] For example, in one case the requesting spouse received Social Security income. On the original joint return, the Social Security income was reported as nontaxable. When the nonrequesting spouse's business expenses were disallowed, the requesting spouse's Social Security income became partially taxable due to the increased income on the joint return. In this case, the requesting spouse would receive a more favorable allocation of liability under subsection (b) or (f) than under subsection (c). *See infra* Chapter 6, II.A.2 (*Attributing the Liability*).

In satisfying the elements of § 6015(c), the taxpayer has the burden to prove marital status and that a portion of the deficiency is attributable to the nonrequesting spouse.[11] The IRS has the burden of proof on the issue of knowledge. Section 6015(c) requires that the IRS prove that the nonrequesting spouse had actual knowledge of the item giving rise to the deficiency.[12]

If a taxpayer becomes eligible to make a claim under § 6015(c) after the Form 8857 is filed, the taxpayer can add an election for relief under § 6015(c).[13]

II. You Win, But You Lose: Considerations When the IRS Grants Relief Under 6015(c) and Denies Relief Under 6015(b)

While it is usually beneficial if the IRS grants spousal relief, sometimes the IRS grants relief under subsection (c) when the requesting spouse might qualify for relief under subsection (b). What difference does it make? If relief is granted under subsection (b), a taxpayer is entitled to refunds, subject to the provisions of § 6015(g), but if relief is granted under subsection (c), the statute bars the requesting spouse from recovering a refund.[14]

Consider this scenario:

> Ron, a self-employed truck driver, and Linda, a waitress, were married and lived together until May 2016, when Linda moved out because Ron was physically abusive. At this time, she obtained an order of protection. After the tax year ended, they filed a joint return because Linda thought married couples were required to file a joint return. In July 2017, they were divorced. Later in 2017, the IRS informed Ron and Linda that they owed additional taxes for 2016 because Ron failed to report $14,000 in income from three Forms 1099. Linda maintains that she had no knowledge of the unreported income. Ron had reported $30,000 in self-employment income on the return and this amount was similar to the income he reported in earlier years. The IRS ultimately assessed $6,000 in additional taxes and took Linda's next two refunds. Each

---

[11] The allocation rules of subsection (c) are strict, except in cases of fraud. If the deficiency is attributable to the requesting spouse and some level of abuse or coercion short of fraud is present, it may be advantageous to focus your efforts on a claim for equitable relief. *See* Rev. Proc. 2013-34, § 4.01(7)(d).

[12] I.R.C. § 6015(c)(3)(C); King v. Comm'r, 116 T.C. 198, 204 (2001); Cheshire v. Comm'r, 115 T.C. 183, 195 (2000), *aff'd*, 282 F.3d 326 (5th Cir. 2002). In ruling against the IRS in Richard v. Comm'r, T.C. Memo. 2011-144, the court held that actual knowledge could not be inferred from circumstantial evidence. Rather, "an actual and clear awareness" is required. Armour v. Comm'r, T.C. Memo. 2016-129, at 10–11. *See also* Treas. Reg. § 1.6015-3(c)(2).

[13] *See* Deihl v. Comm'r, 134 T.C. 162 (2010); Vetrano v. Comm'r, 116 T.C. 272 (2001).

[14] I.R.C. § 6015(g)(3).

refund was primarily due to the earned income tax credit and was for approximately $2,500.

Linda filed a Form 8857 claiming innocent spouse relief under all three subsections of § 6015. She indicated that she had no knowledge of the items of omitted income, that she did not live with Ron for the last seven months of 2016 and that she was physically abused during their marriage. The IRS issued a final determination letter denying relief under § 6015(b), but granted relief under § 6015(c). The final determination letter also indicated that no refunds were allowable because relief was granted under § 6015(c). Thus, if no further action is taken, Linda will not have to pay the balance due ($1,000), but she will not be able to recover a refund for the two refunds totaling $5,000 which were taken and applied to the joint tax liability.

When relief is granted under subsection (c) but denied under (b), the crucial issue is whether a reasonable person in Linda's position would have "had reason to know" of the unreported income. By denying relief under § 6015(b), the IRS position must be that Linda either knew or had reason to know of the understatement. But, by granting relief under § 6015(c), the IRS concedes it does not have proof that Linda had actual knowledge of the omitted income. Combining these two positions leaves the IRS advocating the fragile position that at the time Linda signed the return, she had reason to know, but not actual knowledge, that there was an understatement.[15]

So what can be done? If you are satisfied that Linda did not have reason to know, then you can file a petition with the Tax Court for a redetermination of the denial of relief under § 6015(b). Once the petition is filed, you can use informal discovery and, if necessary, formal discovery to support Linda's claim that she is entitled to relief under subsection (b).[16] In addition to requesting the full administrative file, you can specifically ask the IRS what information it possesses that shows that Linda knew or had reason to know that Ron failed to report income.[17] You already know that the IRS does not possess proof of actual knowledge, because if they did, they would have denied relief under § 6015(c). Requesting the IRS to disclose information in its possession that Linda had reason to know will expose any weaknesses in the IRS position on knowledge.

The recent Taxpayer First Act changes to the Tax Court's scope of review must be considered in litigating Linda's case.[18] The IRS will likely argue

---

[15] Compare, I.R.C. § 6015(b)(1)(C) *with* 6015(c)(3)(C).
[16] *See infra* Chapter 11, II (*Discovery*).
[17] Among the documents that you should look for is the "Appeals Transmittal and Case Memo."
[18] *See supra* Chapter 1, VI (*The Taxpayer First Act of 2019*).

that Linda is prohibited by the administrative record rule from presenting any new evidence in response to the information you receive in discovery.[19] However, as no discovery or cross examination of witnesses was available to Linda in the administrative proceeding, one might argue that Linda's testimony (or other evidence) in response to new information is "newly discovered or previously unavailable".[20]

If the IRS contends that a reasonable person should have known that Ron was underreporting his income, you can offer Linda's testimony to prove that a reasonable person in her circumstances would not have known of the omission. Linda will testify that she was physically abused, moved out of the house in May of 2016 and had very poor communications with Ron for the remainder of the year.[21] She will further testify that she had no knowledge of the omitted income. Thus, in contrast to the IRS's hypothetical person who had reason to know, you can put a credible witness on the stand, subject to the Court's interpretation of § 6015(e)(7)(B). In Linda's case, such an effort can mean the return of $5,000 plus interest.[22]

III. Watch Out for a Tax Benefit in Section 6015(c) Cases

During 2015, your client was employed at the local university. His spouse was self-employed, operating a spa in which your client was not involved. He did not keep the books and records and did not sign checks. A part time bookkeeper maintained the books and records for the spa.

On their 2015 joint return, the couple reported your client's wage income of $38,000 and a net loss from the spa of $40,000 from a Schedule C business (gross revenues of $25,000 and expenses of $65,000), resulting in a taxable income of $0. When the 2015 joint return was filed, the couple received a refund of $4,500, almost all of which was from tax withheld from your client's wages.

In 2017, the IRS audited the 2015 return and disallowed $30,000 of expenses from the operation of the spa. This resulted in a corresponding

---

[19] I.R.C. § 6015(e)(7). Legal arguments can always be made, of course, emphasizing the Court's de novo standard of review.

[20] I.R.C. 6015(e)(7)(B); *see also* Fatty v. Comm'r, No. 3787-20S, 2021 WL 1720004 (U.S. Tax Court Bench Op. Mar. 16, 2021) (nonprecedential) (finding a petitioner's testimony to be "newly available" evidence when he was unable to give sworn testimony when he applied for innocent spouse relief, and neither he nor his wife had been subject to cross-examination during the administrative proceedings).

[21] The Court will place the reasonably prudent person in the particular circumstances of the taxpayer. *See* Aude v. Comm'r, T.C. Memo. 1997-478, (holding that a spouse living in a household in which the other spouse's conduct was threatening and intimidating to her met her duty of inquiry even though she did not review the returns or make inquiries).

[22] *See* Simmons v. Comm'r, T.C. Summ. Op. 2009-6; *see also* Taft v. Comm'r, T.C. Memo. 2017-66; *but see* Culver v. Comm'r, 116 T.C. 189 (2001).

increase in taxable income. The IRS issued a notice of a deficiency asserting a deficiency of $4,000. Prior to your representation, the client filed a *pro se* petition in the Tax Court and raised innocent spouse relief as an affirmative defense. The couple is now divorced.

Consider first whether your client is entitled to relief under § 6015(c). He meets the basic requirements—he is divorced from the nonrequesting spouse and the IRS concedes he did not have actual knowledge of the items. So is it safe to assume that relief will be granted? No.

The IRS will deny relief under § 6015(c) to the extent the requesting spouse received a tax benefit from the understatement of income. Section 6015(d)(1)(B) requires the IRS to allocate an item to a requesting spouse if the item gave rise to a tax benefit for the requesting spouse. When your client filed a joint return, the return included a net loss of $40,000 from the spa, which reduced taxable income, and the tax owed, to zero. But if your client had filed a separate return, he would have owed additional taxes of approximately $4,000. Thus, the IRS is entitled to deny separation of liability relief to the extent that the taxpayer received a benefit from the disallowed item.[23] Your client should instead argue for relief under § 6015(b) or (f).

---

[23] *See also* Reg. § 1.6015-3(d). Significant amendments to this section of the regulations were proposed in 2015. *See* Dept. of the Treasury, *Relief From Joint and Several Liability*, REG-134219-08, 80 Fed. Reg. 72,649, 72,653-54 (Nov. 20, 2015). The discussion is worth reading if your case involves the tax benefit rule.

Chapter 6: Section 6015(f)

I. The Elements of Section 6015(f)—Equitable Relief

Section 6015(f) requires the IRS to consider all relevant facts and circumstances and determine whether it is inequitable to hold the requesting spouse liable for the unpaid tax or deficiency. Partial relief is explicitly available.[1] This is the only form of relief available in underpayment cases.

Equitable relief is limited to cases where relief is not available under subsections (b) and (c).[2] If a claim is made for relief under subsection (b) or (c), the IRS will also consider whether the taxpayer is eligible for relief under subsection (f), even if the taxpayer has not requested such relief.

Relief must be requested within the collection period under section 6502, or within the time for claiming a refund under § 6511.[3]

II. Revenue Procedure 2013-34—Guidelines for Equitable Relief

Section 6015(f) is a broad grant of equitable discretion, so the Commissioner has adopted guidelines to promote uniform review by Service

---

[1] I.R.C. § 6015(f)(1).
[2] I.R.C. § 6015(f)(1)(B).
[3] I.R.C. § 6015(f)(2).

employees. The current guidelines are found in Revenue Procedure 2013-34.[4]

A comparison of the IRS guidelines over the years makes clear how much the IRS's view of innocent spouse relief changed between 1998 and 2013. The 2013 changes overwhelmingly favor the taxpayers who claim equitable relief. The changes include reducing the importance of actual knowledge, giving more weight to abuse and financial control and, finally, abandoning the two-year statute of limitations in equitable relief cases in favor of the 10-year collection statute.

Representatives should study the guidelines. First, experience has shown that IRS examiners sometimes err in applying the guidelines and often an informed advocate can successfully oppose the denial of relief.[5] Second, for claims submitted after July 1, 2019 it is crucial to maximize the record for judicial review by submitting all potentially relevant evidence at the administrative level.[6] Thus, a good understanding of the revenue procedure will protect your client's interests.

Revenue Procedure 2013-34 provides a road map for preparing and filing equitable relief claims. If the client satisfies the threshold conditions, then the revenue procedure sets out guidelines detailing the factors that the IRS will consider. This sounds easy, but the guidelines are complicated because many of the rules have exceptions or nuances. The devil is often in the details. For example, Revenue Procedure 2013-34 § 4.01(7) generally prohibits granting relief when the item generating the liability is attributable to the requesting spouse. But § 4.01(7)(a) through (e) then set out five exceptions to this rule, including if spousal abuse was present. Thus, a thorough understanding of Revenue Procedure 2013-34 is essential to effective representation.

IRS employees will follow Revenue Procedure 2013-34, as will IRS Counsel in Tax Court cases. However, be aware that revenue procedures are not entitled to any judicial deference.[7] Most Tax Court judges will

---

[4] Rev. Proc. 2013-34, 2013-43 IRB 397. The Commissioner had previously issued guidance for equitable relief claims in 2000 and 2003. *See* Rev. Proc. 2000-15, 2000-1 C.B. 447, *superseded by* Rev. Proc. 2003-61, 2003-2 C.B. 296. After ten years of intense litigation the 2003 guidelines were superseded as to § 6015(f) claims by the current revenue procedure. *See supra* Chapter 1, IV (*Innocent Spouse Relief Enters an Era of Intense Litigation*).

[5] In one case, the language in the divorce decree regarding taxes was not sufficient to shift responsibility to the nonrequesting spouse. The IRS insisted that the absence of the shifting language should result in a factor favoring the IRS. After the taxpayer's representative pointed out that the factor should be neutral under the guidelines, Appeals conceded the case.

[6] *See* I.R.C. § 6015(e)(7); *see supra* Chapter 1, VI (*The Taxpayer First Act*).

[7] *See, e.g.*, Williams v. Comm'r, T.C. Memo. 2015-198; *see also* IRS Chief Counsel Notice CC-2019-006 (affirming, *inter alia*, that subregulatory guidance does not have the force of law and the IRS will not argue for judicial deference).

consider the factors and the analysis laid out in Revenue Procedure 2013-34 for their persuasive value, but this is not required.

A. Seven Threshold Conditions

1. In General

Before the IRS will consider equitable relief, Revenue Procedure 2013-34 requires a taxpayer to satisfy seven threshold conditions:

1. The requesting spouse filed a joint return for the taxable year.[8]
2. Relief is not available under section 6015(b) or (c).[9]
3. The claim for relief was timely filed.[10] This has two parts:
    a. Claims for equitable relief from an outstanding liability may be made during the statutory collection period.[11] This is generally a ten-year period, but there can be extensions.
    b. If the collection statute has expired, a claim for refund can be made, subject to the same limitation periods as other tax refund claims.[12]
4. No assets were transferred between the spouses as part of a fraudulent scheme.[13]
5. The nonrequesting spouse did not transfer disqualified assets to the requesting spouse.[14]
6. The requesting spouse did not knowingly participate in the filing of a fraudulent joint return.[15]
7. Generally, the income tax liability for which the requesting spouse seeks relief must be attributable to an item of the nonrequesting spouse.

2. Attributing the Liability

There are five exceptions to the seventh threshold condition. First, if the attribution of income is solely due to the operation of community property laws, the item is considered attributable to the nonrequesting spouse.[16]

---

[8] Rev. Proc. 2013-34, § 4.01(1).
[9] *Id.* § 4.01(2).
[10] *Id.* § 4.01(3).
[11] I.R.C. § 6502.
[12] I.R.C. § 6511.
[13] Rev. Proc. 2013-34, § 4.01(4). In *Hudgins*, the Court denied relief, finding that the taxpayer took affirmative steps to minimize her ownership of assets. She transferred assets as part of a fraudulent scheme. Hudgins v. Comm'r, T.C. Memo. 2012-260.
[14] Rev. Proc. 2013-34, § 4.01(5).
[15] *Id.* § 4.01(6).
[16] Rev. Proc. 2013-34, § 4.01(7)(a); Nunez v. Comm'r, T.C. Memo. 2012-121.

Second, ownership in name only will not preclude relief. If the property is titled in the name of the requesting spouse, there is a rebuttable presumption that the item is attributable to the requesting spouse.[17] Third, if funds intended for the payment of the tax were misappropriated by the nonrequesting spouse, the requesting spouse can be granted relief to the extent of the misappropriation.[18] Fourth, if there was spousal abuse prior to the time the return was filed and the requesting spouse was not able to challenge the treatment of an item on the return, relief can be granted for an item attributable to the requesting spouse.[19] Fifth, an item will be attributed to the nonrequesting spouse if that person's fraud is the reason for the erroneous item.[20]

B. Streamlined Review—Section 4.02

Under Revenue Procedure 2013-34 § 4.02, the IRS provides a faster approval of relief in certain cases. Three elements are considered in a streamlined review:

1. Marital Status. The requesting spouse is legally separated, living apart or divorced. Death of the spouse also satisfies this factor.
2. Economic Hardship. The taxpayer will suffer an economic hardship if the IRS does not grant relief from the income tax liability.
3. Knowledge or Reason to Know. The requesting spouse had no knowledge or reason to know that the liability would not be paid, or that tax was understated on the return.

C. Factors for Determining Equitable Relief—Section 4.03

If the requesting spouse does not qualify for streamlined relief, the IRS will consider the claim under the broader guidelines in § 4.03. Consistent with the statutory requirement to consider all relevant facts and circumstances, Revenue Procedure 2013-34 provides that the factors listed in § 4.03 are not intended to comprise an exclusive list. Importantly, the introductory paragraph to § 4.03 indicates that abuse or financial control by the nonrequesting spouse is a circumstance that may impact other factors.

The nonexclusive factors are:

- Marital Status
- Economic Hardship

---

[17] Rev. Proc. 2013-34, § 4.01(7)(b); Deihl v. Comm'r, T.C. Memo. 2012-176.

[18] Rev. Proc. 2013-34, § 4.01(7)(c); Agudelo v. Comm'r, T.C. Memo. 2015-124.

[19] Rev. Proc. 2013-34, § 4.01(7)(d); Deihl v. Comm'r, T.C. Memo. 2012-176.

[20] Rev. Proc. 2013-34, § 4.01(7)(e); Gebman v. Comm'r, T.C. Memo. 2017-184. "To qualify for equitable relief under section 6015(f). In the Tax Court, the attribution condition is not as strict. See Boyle v. Comm'r, T.C. Memo. 2016-87, 11 (analogizing deceit to fraud, and collecting cases).

- Knowledge or Reason to Know
- Legal Obligation
- Significant Benefit
- Compliance with the Income Tax Laws
- Mental or Physical Health

It is always important to determine if the IRS considered all relevant factors. Occasionally the IRS fails to consider one or more factors, and the Tax Court has criticized the IRS for this omission on at least two occasions.[21]

D. Discussion of Section 4.03 Factors

1. Marital Status[22]

As of the date the Service makes its determination,[23] if the requesting spouse is widowed, divorced, legally separated, or has been living apart from the nonrequesting spouse for at least twelve months, this factor favors relief. Otherwise, this factor is neutral.[24] The guidelines provide that a requesting spouse is a member of the same household as the nonrequesting spouse for any period that they live in the same residence.[25]

2. Economic Hardship[26]

Economic hardship exists if collection of the tax liability in whole or in part will cause the requesting spouse to be unable to pay for basic living expenses.[27]

Under Revenue Procedure 2013-34, the IRS divides economic hardship into two groups based upon the claimants' income. Certain taxpayers are

---

[21] *See* Nihiser v. Comm'r, T.C. Memo. 2008-135 (noting that the IRS failed to consider marital status and abuse); Rosenthal v. Comm'r, T.C. Memo. 2004-89 (noting that the IRS failed to consider six of the eight factors listed in Rev. Proc. 2000-15).

[22] This factor will favor relief or will be neutral. Rev. Proc. 2013-34, § 4.03(2)(a).

[23] Rev. Prof. 2013-34 § 4.03(2)(a); Henson v. Comm'r, T.C. Memo 2012-288, 21. Because the factors are nonexclusive, the Tax Court may consider changes in a spouse's marital situation between the time of the IRS determination and the trial. Often the trial is held a year or more after the IRS determination.

[24] Keitz v. Comm'r, T.C. Memo. 2004-74; *see also* Ewing II, 122 T.C. 32 (2004) (stating that the factor can be neutral where parties are still married and living together). This case was vacated on unrelated jurisdictional grounds by Ewing III, 439 F.3d 1009 (9th Cir. 2006).

[25] Rev. Proc. 2013-34, § 4.03(2)(a). The IRS will not accept the argument that two spouses who live in separate areas of the same residence are maintaining separate residences for innocent spouse purposes. However, advocates are free to argue to the Tax Court that this distinction matters in the circumstances of their case.

[26] This factor will favor relief or will be neutral. Prior to Revenue Procedure 2013-34, it was rare for this factor to be neutral. *See* Martinez v. Comm'r, T.C. Summ. Op. 2008. But the current guidance expressly provides that if denying relief will not cause the requesting spouse an economic hardship, this factor is neutral. Rev. Proc. 2013-34, § 4.03(2)(b).

[27] Rev. Proc. 2013-34, § 4.03(2)(b); *see also* Treas. Reg. § 301.6343-1(b)(4).

entitled to a presumption that collection will cause an economic hardship and these taxpayers do not have to prove their living expenses.[28]

a. Claimants Whose Income Is Under 250% of the Federal Poverty Guidelines

First, the IRS will compare the requesting spouse's income to the federal poverty guidelines.[29] If the requesting spouse's monthly income is below 250% of the federal poverty guidelines, the requesting spouse does not have to prove living expenses and the factor will generally be treated as favoring relief. If the requesting spouse has assets, the IRS will also consider whether the assets can be used to make payments on the taxes and still allow the requesting spouse to cover their basic living expenses.

The poverty guidelines are graduated for different family sizes. The revenue procedure does not define family size for innocent spouse purposes, but the IRS generally defaults to considering the number of people on one's most recent tax return as one's family size.[30] Obviously, this does not always accurately reflect a person's financial obligations, and representatives may need to argue for a different calculation.

b. Claimants Whose Income Is Above 250% of the Federal Poverty Guidelines

Taxpayers with incomes above 250% of the federal poverty guidelines must prove their basic living expenses to win the hardship factor. Care must be taken, because by not offering documentary proof of the client's basic living expenses, this factor may be treated as neutral, which would weaken your client's case for relief. Records of monthly expenses for housing, transportation, medical and other basic living expenses should be gathered, organized, and submitted with Form 8857. If the matter goes to trial, the documents should be included in the stipulation of facts and the requesting spouse should testify about each category.[31] In *Cullen v. Commissioner*,[32] the taxpayer lost this factor by failing to provide sufficient information. No reason exists for failing to prove the basic living expenses of someone

---

[28] Rev. Proc. 2013-34, § 4.03(2)(b).

[29] The federal poverty guidelines are published annually in the Federal Register by the Department of Health and Human Services. They are available online at https://aspe.hhs.gov/poverty-guidelines.

[30] *See* Local Standards, I.R.M. 5.15.1.10 (07-24-2019).

[31] The Tax Court has not yet decided the impact of the administrative record rule on such testimony. If the requesting spouse's financial situation has changed since the IRS made its determination, evidence of hardship may be "previously unavailable" and thus admissible at trial. *See supra* Chapter 1, VI (*The Taxpayer First Act of 2019*).

[32] T.C. Memo. 2004-176.

who is in fact spending their income on basic living expenses, even if they are relatively high income earners.[33]

c. *Safe Harbor for High Income Taxpayers*

If the requesting spouse's income exceeds 250% of the Federal poverty line, this factor will still favor relief if the requesting spouse's monthly income exceeds his or her basic living expenses by $300 or less.

3. Knowledge or Reason to Know[34]

The knowledge factor is a complicated factor. The guidance applies separate tests to understatement cases and underpayment cases.

a. *Understatement Cases*

In an understatement or deficiency case, the knowledge test is whether the requesting spouse knew or had reason to know of the item giving rise to the deficiency. If the requesting spouse did not know or have reason to know, the factor will weigh in favor of relief.

Under IRS guidelines, the weight given to actual knowledge has diminished over time.[35] Revenue Procedure 2013-34 provides that knowledge "will not be weighed more heavily than any other factor."[36] However, knowledge remains an important factor in the eyes of many Tax Court judges,[37] who are not bound by the revenue procedure.

In evaluating reason to know, the guidelines require the IRS to consider the requesting spouse's education, any deceit or evasiveness by the

---

[33] In *Alioto v. Comm'r*, the Tax Court granted relief from approximately $2,000,000 in tax liabilities to a high-income taxpayer based on its findings that the requesting spouse would suffer an economic hardship even though she had an excess of $100,000 in annual salary, $7,000 in savings and $90,000 in a retirement account. Alioto v. Comm'r, T.C. Memo. 2008-185.

[34] This factor will either be awarded to the requesting spouse or to the IRS. Rev. Proc. 2013-34, § 4.03(c)(i)(A), (ii). In some cases, particularly preceding the 2013 guidance, courts have found the factor neutral.

[35] Under Revenue Procedure 2000-15, actual knowledge was first viewed as "an extremely strong factor weighing against relief." Rev. Proc. 2000-15, 2000-1 C.B. 447. Under Revenue Procedure 2003-61, the weight of actual knowledge was reduced to some degree with actual knowledge being treated as a strong factor weighing against relief. Rev. Proc. 2003-61, 2003-2 C.B. 296. But, actual knowledge could be overcome or defeated by the presence of compelling equitable factors. *See* Foor v. Comm'r, T.C. Memo. 2004-54.

[36] Rev. Proc. 2013-34, § 4.03(c)(i)(A).

[37] In some cases the knowledge factor alone has caused the taxpayer to lose relief, despite several positive factors present. *See, e.g.*, Jacobsen v. Comm'r, 950 F.3d 414 (7th Cir. 2020) *and* Sleeth v. Comm'r, 991 F.3d 1201 (11th Cir. 2021) (affirming the denial of relief where the Tax Court had emphasized knowledge over other factors).

nonrequesting spouse, lack of involvement in the nonrequesting spouse's business, and other matters.[38]

b. *Underpayment Cases*

The test for knowledge in an underpayment case is whether the requesting spouse knew or had reason to know at the time the return was filed that the nonrequesting spouse would not pay the income tax liability.[39] In *Washington v. Commissioner*,[40] the Tax Court found credible a taxpayer's testimony that she believed her husband would pay the tax since the tax resulted from his business and he had a history of paying the taxes relating to his business. In many cases, the nonrequesting spouse has assured the requesting spouse that they would take care of the payment.

c. *Abuse and Knowledge*

The revenue procedure explicitly incorporates consideration of abuse into the knowledge factor.[41] If the requesting spouse establishes that they were the victim of abuse to a degree that it interfered with their ability to question or challenge items on the joint return or how the balance due would be paid, the abuse may result in the knowledge factor being awarded to the requesting spouse.[42] If abuse is present, the knowledge factor can be awarded to the requesting spouse even if they had actual knowledge of the item. In addition, the nonrequesting spouse's alcohol abuse or drug abuse can be considered abuse of the requesting spouse in the decision process.[43] Finally, other conduct by the nonrequesting spouse, for example, abuse of the requesting spouse's child, can also be considered as part of the abuse determination.[44]

---

[38] The Tax Court has refused to find constructive knowledge where the nonrequesting spouse concealed income from the requesting spouse. *See* Korchak v. Comm'r, T.C. Memo. 2006-185; Neal v. Comm'r, T.C. Memo. 2005-201, *aff'd*, 557 F.3d 1262 (11th Cir. 2009); *see also supra* Chapter 3, II (*Duty of Inquiry*).

[39] Rev. Proc. 2013-34, § 4.03(c)(ii); *see* Hopkins v. Comm'r, 121 T.C. 73, 88 (2003).

[40] 120 T.C. 137, 151 (2003).

[41] Rev. Proc. 2013-34, § 4.03(c)(iv).

[42] Thomassen v. Comm'r, T.C. Memo. 2011-88, 28. The court found that the requesting spouse had reason to know of the items giving rise to the deficiencies, but "in line with the revenue procedure" in effect at the time, court held that the years of psychological abuse inflicted by the nonrequesting spouse caused the knowledge factor to be neutral. Under the 2013 revenue procedure, the factor would be positive rather than neutral.

[43] Rev. Proc. 2013-34, § 4.03(c)(iv).

[44] *Id.*

4. Legal Obligation to Pay the Tax[45]

If a divorce or legally binding separation agreement places the sole responsibility for paying the tax on the nonrequesting spouse, this factor will generally favor granting relief. However, the factor will be neutral if the requesting spouse knew or had reason to know at the time the divorce or separation agreement was entered that the nonrequesting spouse would not pay the tax.[46] Conversely, if the sole responsibility for paying the tax is placed on the requesting spouse, this factor will weigh against relief. If the spouses remain married or the documents relating to the separation or divorce are silent on the tax issue, this factor will be neutral.

Though neither the IRS nor the Tax Court are bound by a state court order shifting responsibility for the tax, considerable weight may be given to this factor.[47] If the requesting spouse is going through a divorce or separation, it may be helpful to discuss this issue with the client's family law attorney, who may be able to include language in the separation agreement or divorce decree assigning responsibility for the tax to the nonrequesting spouse.

5. Significant Benefit[48]

If the requesting spouse received a significant benefit from the unpaid tax or the deficiency, this factor will weigh against relief. A significant benefit turns on whether the requesting spouse received a benefit beyond normal support.[49]

Under the IRS guidelines, if the nonrequesting spouse significantly benefited from the unpaid tax and the requesting spouse does not benefit, this factor will favor relief.[50] Finally, if the requesting spouse received a benefit beyond normal support, for example expensive vacations, but the nonrequesting spouse controlled the household finances, this factor can be treated as neutral. This is consistent with the case law.[51]

---

[45] This factor can weigh in favor of relief, weigh against relief, or be neutral. Rev. Proc. 2013-34, § 4.03(d).

[46] *Id.*

[47] Pullins v. Comm'r, 136 T.C. 432, 450 (2011).

[48] This factor can weigh in favor of relief, weigh against relief, or be neutral. Rev. Proc. 2013-34, § 4.03(e); *see also* Treas. Reg. § 1.6015–2(d).

[49] *See* Billings v. Comm'r, T.C. Memo. 2007-234 (finding no significant benefit beyond normal support where the couple had a legitimate income of $100,000 and the amounts spent on the requesting spouse and the children were not "significant"). *But see* Stennett-Bailey v. Comm'r, T.C. Memo. 2011-250 (denying the requesting spouse this factor because at a time when she knew of the tax debt, she used monies from a joint account to pay the mortgage on her residence, to pay expenses of her vacation home, and to pay for private tuition).

[50] Rev. Proc. 2013-34, § 4.03(e).

[51] *See* Ewing II, 122 T.C. 32, 45 (2004), *vacated on unrelated jurisdictional grounds*, Ewing III, 439 F.3d 1009 (9th Cir. 2006).

The IRS has at times argued the position that if the requesting spouse received a portion of a refund due to the earned income credit, a significant benefit was received regardless of the requesting spouse's economic circumstances.[52]

The guidelines contain an unusual rule: "If the amount of the tax or understatement was small such that neither spouse received a significant benefit, then this factor is neutral." This seems to undercut the general rule that the factor would be favorable if the nonrequesting spouse did not receive a benefit beyond normal support. While this is the IRS's stated position, the Tax Court has rejected it in several cases.[53]

6. Compliance with the Income Tax Laws[54]

Compliance with the tax laws after the year in controversy is important because the requesting spouse's failure to meet their tax filing and payment obligations can undermine their claim for equitable relief. The IRS analyzes this factor differently for each tax year depending on whether the requesting spouse was still married to the nonrequesting spouse, and if so, whether returns were filed jointly or separately. If the requesting spouse filed separately and made a good faith effort to comply but has been unable to fully comply due to financial hardship or other reasons, the factor will be neutral.[55]

While this is a relatively straightforward factor, it requires coordination with the taxpayer from the moment the attorney client relationship is established. For example, if the client wants to make a claim for innocent spouse relief for 2019 and meets with an attorney in March of 2022, the failure to file timely for 2021 may be enough to lose this factor. Thus, the representative must pay attention to whether the requesting spouse is filing his or her returns annually and paying the tax due. A client may contend that their divorce attorney or accountant told them not to file future returns until their prior liabilities were resolved. Or the client may be under the mistaken belief that if they don't file a joint return, they can't file at all. Since many innocent spouse cases last for a year or more, the representative needs to pay attention to this issue each year.

At the first meeting, the representative should review the client's filing history and should advise the client about the importance of complying with the

---

[52] *See supra* Chapter 4, II (*Refundable Credits and Substantial Benefit*); *see also* Rosenthal v. Comm'r, TC. Memo. 2004-89 (noting that significant benefit and economic hardship are separate and distinct factors).

[53] Boyle v. Comm'r, T.C. Memo. 2016-87; Hollimon v. Comm'r, T.C. Memo. 2015-157; Howerter v. Comm'r, T.C. Summ. Op. 2014-15.

[54] This factor can weigh in favor of relief, weigh against relief, or be neutral. Rev. Proc. 2013-34, § 4.03(f).

[55] *Id.* at § 4.03(f)(i), (iii). The factor cannot be neutral for a certain tax year if a joint return was filed. *Id.* at § 4.03(f)(ii).

tax laws, filing timely returns, and paying all future taxes. It may be a good idea to include the language regarding the client's duty to file subsequent year returns in a letter to the client. If the client fails to file returns and the IRS can establish lack of compliance, the court may award this factor to the IRS, thereby reducing the chance of qualifying for equitable relief.[56] If the taxpayer fails to offer proof of compliance, this factor can be treated as neutral.[57]

7. Mental or Physical Health[58]

This is an important factor. The existence of mental or physical health issues increases the likelihood the Tax Court will view the totality of the circumstances as warranting equitable relief.[59]

Many taxpayers have serious physical and mental health issues that impact their daily lives. The compound impact of health issues with other issues, such as economic hardship, can make a very compelling case for equitable relief. The absence of this factor is treated as neutral.

III. All of the Facts and Circumstances

Section 6015(f) provides that in making a determination the Commissioner shall take into account all the facts and circumstances. The guidance mirrors this language, noting that the factors "are designed as guides and not intended to comprise an exclusive list," and that "other factors relevant to a specific claim may also be taken into account."[60]

Representatives must be assertive in identifying and explaining additional circumstances that impact the ultimate question: whether it would be inequitable to hold the requesting spouse liable for the tax. For example, in *Denton v. Commissioner*, the Tax Court considered two positive unlisted factors: (1) the requesting spouse's income was so low during the tax year at issue that she had no filing obligation on her own; and (2) most of the liability consisted of the other spouse's self-employment tax under I.R.C. § 1401.[61] Conversely, in *Sutherland v. Commissioner* the Court considered additional negative facts: (1) the requesting spouse expected a sizable inheritance at the time she signed the returns; and (2) at the time she filed

---

[56] Pullins v. Comm'r, 136 T.C. 432 (2011).

[57] Geaccone v. Comm'r, T.C. Summ. Op. 2007-58; Bennett v. Comm'r, T.C. Summ. Op. 2005-84.

[58] This factor will either weigh in favor of relief or be neutral. Rev. Proc. 2013-34, § 4.03(g).

[59] *See* August v. Comm'r, T.C. Memo. 2002-201.

[60] Rev. Proc. 2013-34, § 4.03(2).

[61] Denton v. Comm'r, T.C. Summ. Op. 2009-87. The latter fact may be especially helpful if the marriage was too short to afford the requesting spouse any Social Security benefits on the nonrequesting spouse's record. A divorced spouse may be eligible for benefits if the marriage lasted at least ten years. *See* 40 C.F.R. § 404.331; *see also* 40 C.F.R. § 404.330-404.349 (*Benefits for Spouses and Divorced Spouses*).

Form 8857, the requesting spouse had over $400,000 in bank accounts and could have easily paid the joint tax liability.[62]

In practice, IRS personnel sometimes resist considering facts and circumstances outside the listed factors.[63] In the event that relief is denied, a thorough understanding of the factors in the revenue procedure will enable the representative to decide whether the examiner considered all the facts and circumstances or just the listed factors. If there has been a failure to consider all of the facts and circumstances, the representative can raise the issue and this may add considerable value to the success of your client's claim.

Historically, in some cases both the IRS and the courts awarded or denied relief based upon a majority of the factors.[64] But the 2013 guidelines moved away from the majority of factors approach, providing that "no one factor or a majority of the factors necessarily determines the outcome."[65] The guidance provides that the importance of each factor will vary depending on the facts and circumstances. For example, one examiner might deny relief to a requesting spouse who established a majority of the factors, if the examiner found that they had actual knowledge at the time the return was filed that the nonrequesting spouse would not pay the tax due shown on the return. But another examiner might grant relief if they did not attribute as much weight to the knowledge factor. Thus, the possibility of inconsistent treatment is obvious.

IV. The Role of Abuse

By far the biggest change made in Revenue Procedure 2013-34 is that the IRS eliminated abuse as an independent factor and instead recognized that abuse and financial control are relevant to many aspects of the equitable relief analysis.[66] If the claimant is a victim of abuse then this can cause certain factors weighing against relief to be counted toward relief. Here are two examples:

1. Knowledge or Reason to Know. If the requesting spouse had knowledge or reason to know of the income item, but they did not question the item because of abuse or fear of retaliation, the factor will be considered favoring relief.[67]

---

[62] Sutherland v. Comm'r, T.C. Memo. 2021-110.

[63] *See* Nihiser v. Comm'r, T.C. Memo. 2008-135; Rosenthal v. Comm'r, T.C. Memo. 2004-89.

[64] For example, in *Zaher v. Comm'r*, T.C. Memo. 2012-11, the court awarded equitable relief, holding three factors favored relief, two factors opposed relief, and three were neutral.

[65] Rev. Proc. 2013-34, § 4.03(2). Indeed, winning a majority of the factors is far from a guarantee of success, especially if the knowledge factor is negative. Keith Fogg, *Knowledge Leaves Another Innocent Spouse Petitioner Standing at the Altar*, Procedurally Taxing (Oct. 1, 2021), https://procedurallytaxing.com/knowledge-leaves-another-innocent-spouse-petitioner-standing-at-the-altar/ [https://perma.cc/V7E7-K7AH].

[66] Rev. Proc. 2013-34, §§ 3.01, 4.03(2).

[67] Rev. Proc. 2013-34, § 4.03(2)(c).

2. Significant Benefit. If the requesting spouse received a significant benefit in excess of normal support, but they had no say in how the household finances were conducted and they were the victim of abuse, the factor will be considered neutral.[68]

Advocates must connect the abusive circumstances to the equitable relief analysis in a compelling way.[69]

A. *Defining Abuse*[70]

Revenue Procedure 2013-34 lists four areas of abuse: 1) physical; 2) psychological; 3) sexual; and 4) emotional. It also includes conduct by the nonrequesting spouse to control, isolate, humiliate, intimidate, and undermine the requesting spouse's ability to make independent decisions under the tax laws.[71] But the guidance goes further. It notes that the nonrequesting spouse's alcohol or drug abuse could be considered as abuse. Finally, the revenue procedure notes that in a given case, abuse of the requesting spouse's child or family member might constitute abuse. Thus, it is apparent that the IRS has made great progress in understanding the nature of abusive relationships.

B. *Income Attributable to the Requesting Spouse and Abuse*

One of the threshold conditions discussed above is whether the liability is attributable to the nonrequesting spouse. Generally, if the income is attributable to the requesting spouse, the IRS can properly deny equitable relief. But if there was abuse in the home and the requesting spouse was not in a position to ask questions about the income tax return, then the IRS may grant relief even though the income is attributable to the requesting spouse.

In *Thomassen v. Commissioner*,[72] the IRS denied relief to the requesting spouse in part because some of the deficiencies were attributable to the requesting spouse. But the court considered whether the requesting spouse

---

[68] Rev. Proc. 2013-34, § 4.03(2)(e).

[69] In *Brigette Ogden v. Comm'r*, T.C. Memo. 2019-88, the Court found that the nonrequesting spouse's abuse of the requesting spouse was not relevant to the equitable relief determination under the circumstances of the case.

[70] For spousal relief purposes, duress and abuse are related but different concepts. Duress relates to the moment the return is signed and exists when a spouse forces his or her spouse to file a joint tax return. *See* Brown v. Comm'r, T.C. Summ. Op. 2008-121. Abuse differs from duress in several respects: 1) unlike a finding of duress, a finding of abuse does not nullify the filing of a joint return; 2) the abusive conduct can be less intimidating than duress; and 3) the abusive conduct can occur either before or after the return was signed. For further discussion of duress, *see supra* Chapter 2, III (*Duress*).

[71] Rev. Proc. 2013-34, § 4.03(3)(iv). Financial control is specifically mentioned in several parts of the revenue procedure.

[72] T.C. Memo. 2011-88.

was the victim of abuse during the marriage to such a degree that she was prevented from meeting her tax obligations. The court found that the nonrequesting spouse had regularly inflicted psychological abuse to such an extent that the court held the requesting spouse could be relieved of items attributable to her.

C. Proving Abuse

As with any factor, documents may carry substantial weight. For example, documents showing that the nonrequesting spouse was convicted of domestic violence against the taxpayer can be compelling. Representatives should seek such documents from their clients and independent sources including police stations, courts, doctors, and hospitals. The following are examples of helpful documents:

- Orders of protection;
- Criminal complaints and/or police reports;
- Court records of criminal proceedings for domestic abuse;
- Photos, x-rays, or other pictures of physical abuse; and
- Affidavits from the requesting spouse, medical providers, and other witnesses.

It is not unusual for documentation of abuse to be sparse. People in abusive relationships can be unable to seek outside help for many years. In that case, it is essential to help your client construct a coherent, compelling narrative that is internally and externally consistent. A detailed, sworn statement can be extremely persuasive if it allows the fact finder to put themselves in your client's shoes. Be creative in seeking external substantiation to the extent possible. But, lack of documents should not dissuade you from telling your client's story.[73]

V. Proving Economic Hardship

As explained above, the economic hardship factor weighs in favor of relief if collection of the tax liability will prevent the taxpayer from paying their reasonable basic living expenses. Taxpayers making more than 250% of the poverty level must prove their basic living expenses.

For those taxpayers who must prove economic hardship, Revenue Procedure 2013-34 directs the reader to Regulation section 301.6343-1(b)(4), which provides that the ability to pay for reasonable basic living expenses involves a consideration of the following nonexclusive factors:

---

[73] *See also infra* Chapter 8, V (*Documenting Domestic Abuse*).

- the taxpayer's age, employment status and history, ability to earn, and number of dependents;
- the amount reasonably necessary for food, clothing, housing, medical expenses, transportation, current tax payments, and expenses necessary to the taxpayer's income producing activity;
- the cost of living in the taxpayer's geographic area;
- the amount of property available to satisfy the taxpayer's expenses;
- any extraordinary circumstances; e.g., special education expenses, medical catastrophe, or a natural disaster; and
- any other factor bearing on economic hardship. The courts have also been willing to consider the taxpayer's retirement needs.

The IRS has issued guidelines for reasonable living expenses.[74] Courts may look to these standards, but the requesting spouse bears the burden of proof. Failing to offer detailed evidence and documents substantiating economic hardship can result in the loss of this factor.[75]

Arguably the economic hardship factor requires more proof (and therefore more effort by the representative) than any other factor. The courts expect documentary evidence substantiating the inability to pay basic living expenses to be introduced into the record. It is not usually enough for the taxpayer to offer self-serving testimony about their monthly income and expenses or to testify that they had special medical expenses of $10,000 for their child. Documents must be produced to corroborate the taxpayer's self-serving testimony. The economic hardship must not be hypothetical, rather the proof must show that collection would pose a present economic hardship.[76]

A representative should work with the client to obtain the following documents:

- Proof of Gross Monthly Income. Recent 3 showing year-to-date earnings, or a self-employed taxpayer's current Profit & Loss statement. If financial statements are unavailable for a self-employed client, a representative can prepare a deposit analysis from the client's bank account statements.

---

[74] IRS, Collection Financial Standards, *available at* https://www.irs.gov/businesses/small-businesses-self-employed/collection-financial-standards (last visited Jan. 30, 2022).

[75] *See* Butner v. Comm'r, T.C. Memo. 2007-136; Ware v. Comm'r, T.C. Memo. 2007-112. In *Schwind v. Comm'r*, the taxpayer failed to substantiate most of her expenses. The Court looked to the IRS's national and local standards and determined that the taxpayer did not face economic hardship. T.C. Summ. Op. 2008-119.

[76] *See* Pullins v. Comm'r, 136 T.C. 432, 446-47 (2011) (hardship was hypothetical where the requesting spouse Ms. Pullins did not offer evidence of what her living expenses would be if she moved out of the house she shared with Mr. Pullins).

- Housing Expenses. Lease agreements, mortgage statements, utility bills, water bills, cell phone bills, homeowner's or renter's insurance premium statements, homeowner association dues statements, and any documentation of home maintenance costs.
- Transportation Expenses. Ownership costs: auto loan statements and lease agreements. Operating costs: auto insurance premiums, registration fees, invoices of maintenance and repairs, and gas receipts. An operating expense figure below the IRS standard is not usually questioned.
- Expenses for Food and Personal Items. If your client's expenses exceed the national standards, ask the client to keep receipts for food and personal items for two to three months.
- Health Care Expenses. Paystubs, tax forms (SSA-1099, 1095-A), or bills showing health insurance premiums.[77] Canceled checks and medical records to show insurance payments and co-pays, summaries of prescriptions from the pharmacies, and letters from health care professionals regarding anticipated future medical expenses.
- Tax Obligations. IRS account transcripts to show subsequent compliance, including estimated payments for the current year. A recent paystub to show year-to-date withholding.
- Court Ordered Payments. Documentation of judgments, alimony and child support obligations, and other court ordered payments.
- Liabilities. In addition to showing monthly income and expenses, it is also helpful to show that the client has substantial liabilities above and beyond his or her tax debts. An effective way to demonstrate a client's debts is to provide a current copy of the client's credit report, as well as copies of recent credit card statements and correspondence demanding payment for overdue bills.
- Retirement Accounts. In considering whether paying the tax would create an economic hardship, the Tax Court has viewed retirement accounts in a favorable light.[78] This issue depends on the facts and circumstances of each case. The representative should prepare and present a thorough argument as to why the taxpayer's retirement funds should not be applied toward the tax liabilities.

---

[77] Older people may pay multiple Medicare premiums. *See* Medicare.gov, https://www.medicare.gov/your-medicare-costs/medicare-costs-at-a-glance [https://perma.cc/59C9-NZX6] (last visited Jan. 30, 2022).

[78] In *Van Arsdalen v. Comm'r*, T.C. Memo. 2007-48, and *Alioto v. Comm'r*, T.C. Memo. 2008-185, the taxpayers had retirement accounts of $63,000 and $99,000, respectively. Nevertheless, in both cases, the court found that payment of the tax would create an economic hardship.

Chapter 7: Community Property States

I. Characteristics of Community Property States

Nine states and two U.S. territories apply community property laws to married couples domiciled in their jurisdictions.[1] In community property states, most property acquired during marriage is owned by the marital community, with each spouse having a vested half interest.[2] State law dictates how and to what extent spouses in community property states can change the ownership of their property and income from community treatment to common law treatment.[3]

---

[1] The community property states are Arizona, California, Idaho, Louisiana, Nevada, New Mexico, Texas, Washington, and Wisconsin. Puerto Rico and Guam are also community property jurisdictions. This chapter does not discuss opt-in community property regimes, as they do not impact federal income tax. *See* Comm'r v. Harmon, 323 U.S. 44 (1944).

[2] *See* Loren E. Mulraine, *Collision Course: State Community Property Laws and Termination Rights Under the Federal Copryight Act-Who Should Have the Right of Way?*, 100 MARQ. L. REV. 1193, 1213 (2017). Each state's law has its own nuances and exceptions to the general rule. *See, e.g.*, Beck v. Comm'r, T.C. Memo. 2001-198, 16 (summarizing Texas law); Bennett v. Comm'r, T.C. Summ. Op. 2005-84, 5 (summarizing California law). The IRM includes a summary of state laws at Exhibit 25.18.1-1, Comparison of State Law Differences in Community Property States.

[3] *See, e.g.*, Tex. Fam. Code Ann. § 3.410; 4.102 (providing, inter alia, that spouses may partition community property by agreement).

Taxpayers' domicile dictates whether community property treatment applies to their earnings and moveable property.[4] In contrast, ownership of real property depends on the law of the state in which the land is situated.[5] A spouse domiciled in Texas (a community property state) but working in neighboring Oklahoma (a common law state) has community property income.[6] Spouses domiciled in Oregon (a common law state) can hold land as community property in Washington (a community property state.)[7]

II. Federal Income Taxation of Community Property

Under U.S. Supreme Court precedent, income from community property is taxed according to its ownership under state law, which generally means it is taxed equally to each spouse.[8] If spouses residing in a community property state file separate tax returns, generally each spouse must report and pay income taxes on half of the community income, regardless of who actually earned or received the income.[9] Because of the harsh results this rule can create, Congress enacted I.R.C. § 66.

III. Impact of Community Property on the Innocent Spouse Relief Under Section 6015

A person residing in a community property state who filed a joint tax return can seek relief from the liability under I.R.C. § 6015. This is possible because community property laws are disregarded when allocating items to determine a requesting spouse's eligibility for relief under I.R.C. § 6015.[10] As discussed in Chapters 3 through 6, innocent spouse relief is generally only available for liabilities caused by income, credits, or deductions attributable to the nonrequesting spouse.

In separation of liability cases under I.R.C. § 6015(c), the IRS if denying relief must establish that the requesting spouse had actual knowledge of the understated item. Joint ownership by operation of community property laws does not imply actual knowledge and so does not prevent relief.[11]

---

[4] Black v. Comm'r, 114 F.2d 355, 359 (9th Cir. 1940); Quintana v. Ordono, 195 So. 2d 577 (Fla. Dist. Ct. App. 1967). *See also* Jeremy T. Ware, *Section 1014(b)(6) and the Boundaries of Community Property*, 5 Nev. L.J. 704, 715-23 (2005) (discussing the impact of changes in domicile between community and common law states).

[5] *Black v. Comm'r*, 114 F.2d at 357-58.

[6] *See* Beck v. Comm'r, T.C. Memo. 2001-198, 16 (noting that a spouse's earnings are community property under Texas law, citing Winger v. Pianka, 831 S.W.2d 853, 857 (Tex. App. 1992)).

[7] *Black v. Comm'r*, 114 F.2d at 357-58.

[8] U.S. v. Mitchell, 403 U.S. 190, 194-97 (1971); Poe v. Seaborn, 282 U.S. 101 (1930).

[9] *Id.*; Treas. Reg. § 1.66-1(a).

[10] Treas. Reg. § 1.6015-1(f).

[11] Treas. Reg. § 1.6015-3(c)(2)(iv); *see, e.g.*, Kitazono v. Comm'r, No. 3961-20 (T.C. Bench Op. Dec. 17, 2021).

Community property laws are not entirely irrelevant to innocent spouse relief, however. If relief is granted, payments made from community property will not be refundable.[12] Only payments made by the requesting spouse from separate property will be refunded.

If a joint return was filed, always consider whether I.R.C. § 6015(b), (c), or (f) could provide relief for your client.

IV. Overview of Relief from Liability Under Section 66

Section 66 offers four exceptions to the default 50/50 taxation of community property income.[13] These exceptions apply when:

- Spouses live apart and meet the requirements of I.R.C. § 66(a);
- The IRS denies the benefit of community property taxation to a spouse who fails to notify the other spouse of community income and meets the requirements of I.R.C. § 66(b);
- A spouse files separately and qualifies for traditional relief under I.R.C. § 66(c); or
- A spouse qualifies for I.R.C. § 66(c) equitable relief under procedures prescribed by the government.

Individuals can apply for or claim the benefits of the first, third, and fourth exceptions to community property taxation, but the second exception, for failure to notify, must be asserted by the IRS. I.R.C. § 66(b) is not a relief provision for the innocent spouse, but rather a sanction for the culpable spouse.[14]

Separate taxation under I.R.C. § 66(a) is claimed by simply filing one's tax return (or an amended return) in accordance with that provision. Your client may be entitled to this treatment if the spouses lived apart all year, did not share their income, and filed separate returns.[15] If the requirements of I.R.C. § 66(a) are met, community income is treated in accordance with I.R.C. § 879(a).[16] This provides for separate taxation of many, but not all, types of income. For example, wages would be taxed separately but capital gains on jointly held property would not.

---

[12] *See* Ordlock v. Comm'r, 533 F.3d 1136 (9th Cir. 2008) (affirming 126 T.C. 47 (2006)).

[13] These are further detailed in regulations at Treas. Reg. §§ 1.66-1 through 1.66-4.

[14] Treas. Reg. § 1.66-3; Hardy v. Comm'r, 181 F.3d 1002, 1007 (9th Cir. 1999) (affirming T.C. Memo. 1997-97).

[15] *See* Treas. Reg. § 1.66-2.

[16] *See* I.R.C. § 879(a)(1)-(a)(4).

Relief under I.R.C. § 66(c) is claimed on Form 8857, following the same procedures as for requesting relief under I.R.C. § 6015.[17] This includes administrative appeal rights.[18]

If relief is granted, the item of community income that is no longer taxable to the requesting spouse will be included in the gross income of the nonrequesting spouse.[19] Because of this, the requesting spouse must cooperate with "reasonable requests" for information to assist the IRS in locating the nonrequesting spouse.[20] The nonrequesting spouse will also receive notice of the request and the opportunity to submit information to the IRS.[21] The regulation states that the IRS "will share" the information submitted by each spouse with the other, unless doing so will impair tax administration. However, the IRM uses permissive rather than mandatory language, and directs employees not to disclose a spouse's new last name, location, phone number, or any information about their employment, income, or assets.[22]

While relief from community property taxation is very similar to innocent spouse relief, there are some notable differences, particularly as to the timing and scope of traditional relief. The two relief provisions in I.R.C. § 66(c) are discussed in more detail below.

V. Traditional Relief Under Section 66(c)

A. The Elements of Traditional Relief

Section § 66(c) provides relief where:

- A joint return was not filed;
- The requesting spouse's tax return failed to report community income that would be allocated to the nonrequesting spouse under I.R.C. § 879(a);
- The requesting spouse did not know or have reason to know of the item of community income;
- Considering all the facts and circumstances, it is inequitable to include the item of community income in the requesting spouse's gross income; and

---

[17] Treas. Reg. § 1.66-4(j); Rev. Proc. 2013-34 § 5. The regulation also allows a claim to be made in writing signed under penalties of perjury, but the IRS prefers to receive Form 8857.

[18] *See* Appeal Rights, I.R.M. 25.15.5.21 (07-24-2017); *see also* Chapter 9, *infra*..

[19] I.R.C. § 66(c) (flush language); Treas. Reg. § 1.66-4(d).

[20] Treas. Reg. § 1.66-4(j)(1).

[21] Treas. Reg. § 1.66-4(k); Notification Requirement, I.R.M. 25.15.5.20 (07-24-2017).

[22] Notification Requirement, I.R.M. 25.15.5.20 (07-24-2017).

- The taxpayer requests relief after being notified of an examination or potential deficiency and at least 6 months prior to the expiration of the assessment period applicable to the nonrequesting spouse, or within 30 days of the IRS commencing to examine the requesting spouse's return, whichever is later.

The requirements of I.R.C. § 66(c) are stated in the conjunctive; each condition must be satisfied. In addition to the elements above, relief is not available if the IRS proves that the spouses transferred assets between them as part of a fraudulent scheme.[23]

B. Discussion

Traditional relief from the operation of community property taxation under I.R.C. § 66(c) is similar to traditional innocent spouse relief under I.R.C. § 6015(b), but it is more limited in certain respects.

First, relief is available for a narrower range of liabilities. Whereas § 6015(b) relief is available for any component of a deficiency, traditional § 66(c) relief can only apply to omitted items of *income*.[24] Deficiencies caused by overstated deductions or credits cannot be relieved by this provision.

Furthermore, the omitted income must qualify to be allocated to the nonrequesting spouse under I.R.C. § 879(a). This requirement barred relief in the case of *Wheeler v. Commissioner*.[25] In *Wheeler*, the petitioner and her husband were the sole shareholders of a jointly operated S corporation. The spouses divorced and the business was awarded to petitioner's husband. The petitioner failed to report any income from the company for the year of the divorce, and the IRS issued a notice of deficiency based on the income reported for her on Schedule K-1. As a threshold matter of eligibility the Tax Court noted that, under § 879(a)(2), business income is treated as provided in I.R.C. § 1402(a)(5). That provision dictates that the income from a jointly operated nonpartnership business is "treated as the gross income … of each spouse on the basis of their respective distributive share …"[26] Because the K-1 had reported only petitioner's share of the income based on her ownership percentage that year, relief was not available to her under I.R.C. § 66(c).

Second, relief under I.R.C. § 66(c) is subject to more complicated time limitations. Whereas § 6015(b) relief must be requested within 2 years of the first collection action on the liability, traditional relief under I.R.C.

---

[23] Treas. Reg. § 1.66-4(f).
[24] *See* Treas. Reg. § 1.66-4(a)(1)(ii).
[25] Wheeler v. Comm'r, T.C. Summ. Op. 2021-42.
[26] I.R.C. § 1402(a)(5)(A).

§ 66(c) may be requested no earlier than the date of the first notice to the requesting spouse of a potential deficiency, and no later than 6 months before the expiration of the assessment period applicable to the nonrequesting spouse.[27] If the IRS begins an examination of the requesting spouse's return during that 6 months, the deadline is 30 days from the commencement of the examination.[28]

As in I.R.C. § 6015 cases, the knowledge factor does not refer to knowledge of the tax law. Knowledge of the activity that produced the income is enough to disqualify a taxpayer from relief.[29]

The equitable inquiry for traditional community property relief is nearly identical to that under § 6015, except for the "benefit" factor.[30] Treasury Regulation § 1.66-4(a)(3) specifies that "normal support" is considered a benefit that is relevant to whether it is inequitable to hold a requesting spouse liable for tax on the nonrequesting spouse's omitted income. This contrasts with § 6015, where only a "significant benefit" above normal support weighs against relief.[31]

VI. Equitable Relief Under I.R.C. Section 66(c)

A. The Elements of Equitable Relief

The flush language of I.R.C. § 66(c) allows the Secretary to grant relief from any unpaid tax or deficiency, if, considering all the facts and circumstances, it is inequitable to hold the requesting spouse liable. Partial relief is explicitly available.

Traditional relief must be considered first. Equitable relief is limited to cases where traditional relief is not available.[32]

Equitable relief from community property taxation is evaluated under the same criteria as equitable relief under I.R.C. § 6015(f).[33]

B. Discussion

Equitable relief is the only option where liability on a separate return is caused by a disallowed deduction or credit, or by an item of community income that would not be allocated to the nonrequesting spouse under I.R.C. § 879(a). For example, capital gains on jointly held property are still taxed 50/50 as community property even under I.R.C. § 879(a).

---

[27] Treas. Reg. § 1.66-4(j)(2)(i).
[28] *Id.*
[29] McGee v. Comm'r, 979 F.2d 66, 70 (5th Cir. 1992) (collecting cases).
[30] *See* Treas. Reg. § 1.66-4(a)(3); Rev. Proc. 2013-34 § 1.
[31] Rev. Proc. 2013-34 § 4.03(2)(e).
[32] I.R.C. § 66(c) (flush language).
[33] Treas. Reg. § 1.66-4(b); Rev. Proc. 2013-34 § 1.01.

The timing restrictions on an equitable relief request are more relaxed than for traditional relief. If the liability concerns a tax deficiency, the earliest time to request relief is when the IRS notifies the requesting spouse of a potential liability.[34] Relief for a self-reported liability may be requested as early as when the tax return is filed.[35] As with I.R.C. § 6015(f), equitable relief is available at any time during the collection period and during the time to claim a refund.[36]

VII. Judicial Review of Relief from Community Property Taxation

A. Introduction

I.R.C. § 66 lacks any provision for judicial review. For this reason, the Tax Court has held that it does not have jurisdiction to consider "standalone" denials of relief under I.R.C. § 66.[37] Also, the nonrequesting spouse has no statutory right to intervene in a judicial proceeding concerning relief from community property taxation. Otherwise, the Tax Court's jurisdiction over community property relief parallels its review of innocent spouse relief asserted under I.R.C. § 6015.[38]

B. Community Property Relief Under the Tax Court's Deficiency Jurisdiction

A denial of separate treatment under I.R.C. § 66(a) will be subject to judicial review under the Tax Court's deficiency jurisdiction, when the government asserts a deficiency in tax.[39] The same is true for a denial of traditional relief under I.R.C. § 66(c). As for equitable relief, the government argued against judicial review in deficiency cases, just as it did for I.R.C. § 6015(f), and it lost.[40] Originally the Tax Court applied an abuse of discretion standard to its review; however, it has not squarely addressed

---

[34] Treas. Reg. § 1.66-4(j)(2)(ii).

[35] *Id.*

[36] Time Period for Filing a Request for Relief, I.R.M. 25.15.5.16 (07-24-2017); *see also infra* Chapter 13, III (*General Rules for all Refunds*).

[37] Bernal v. Comm'r, 120 T.C. 102 (2003).

[38] *See* Beck v. Comm'r, T.C. Memo. 2001-198 (finding de novo review appropriate when equitable relief under I.R.C. § 66(c) is raised as an affirmative defense to a deficiency, and noting that the equitable relief provisions of sections 6015 and 66 were enacted together).

[39] *See generally* I.R.C. §§ 6211 – 6216, *Deficiency Procedures in the Case of Income, Estate, Gift, and Certain Excise Taxes.*

[40] Beck v. Comm'r, T.C. Memo. 2001-198, 21 (*acq.* A.O.D. 2022-005, 2002-49 I.R.B. (Dec. 9, 2002)).

the appropriate standard of review since its decision to apply de novo review to § 6015(f) cases in *Porter v. Commissioner* (*Porter II*).[41]

C. Community Property Relief in Collection Due Process Cases

The Tax Court can consider spousal defenses raised in a Collection Due Process (CDP) appeal, including defenses under I.R.C. § 66(c).[42] For purposes of judicial review there are two categories of CDP cases: those in which the taxpayer has the right to challenge their underlying liability, and those in which the taxpayer does not have that right.[43]

If the underlying liability is properly at issue in a CDP case, the Tax Court makes a de novo determination of the correct tax liability.[44] This can be dangerous territory for petitioners in community property states. In the case of *Shuang-Di Sun Bennett v. Commissioner*, the petitioner challenged her self-reported liability in CDP.[45] She testified that she had been in an abusive marriage at the time she filed her separate return, and the W-2 she received from her then-husband's business showed wages that she had not earned. The Court credited the petitioner's testimony at trial, but the operation of community property laws complicated her path to relief. The Court found that Mrs. Bennett had failed to report half of the community income earned by her husband and proceeded to recalculate her gross income taking California community property law into account. Only after that step did the Court consider whether Mrs. Bennett qualified for any spousal relief. While I.R.C. § 66(c) ultimately benefitted Mrs. Bennett, the court appeal did not reduce her liability to the extent she had hoped.

The standard of review in all other CDP cases is abuse of discretion.[46] The Tax Court decides whether IRS Appeals abused its discretion in rejecting spousal relief (or the taxpayer's other arguments) and in sustaining the lien notice or the proposed levy at issue. In reaching this decision, the Tax

---

[41] Porter v. Comm'r, 132 T.C. 203 (2009) (Porter II); *see also* Felt v. Comm'r, T.C. Memo. 2009-245; Wheeler v. Comm'r, T.C. Summ. Op. 2021-42. The IRS's acquiescence to *Porter II* in the wake of *Wilson v. Comm'r* does not mention community property relief, but the two provisions would be difficult to distinguish. *See* A.O.D. 2012-07, 2013-25 I.R.B. (June 17, 2013). Note that the Taxpayer First Act amended the standard and scope of review for I.R.C. § 6015 cases (codifying *Porter II* and overruling *Porter I* as to those cases), but the legislation did not address § 66. *See supra* Chapter 1, IV.B (*Innocent Spouse Relief Enters an Era of Intense Litigation—Scope of Evidence and Standard of Review*), VI (*The Taxpayer First Act of 2019*), and accompanying footnotes.

[42] Bernal v. Comm'r, 120 T.C. 102 (2003); I.R.C. § 6330(c)(2)(A)(i).

[43] I.R.C. § 6330(c)(2)(B) sets out when a taxpayer may challenge their liability in CDP. For an in-depth discussion of Collection Due Process, see Chapter 10B of Effectively Representing Your Client Before the IRS (ABA 8th Ed. 2021). The chapter is authored by Brian Gardner, Nikki McCain, and Bryant Hinckley.

[44] Goza v. Comm'r, 114 T.C. 176, 181-82 (2000).

[45] T.C. Summ. Op. 2005-84.

[46] Sego v. Comm'r, 114 T.C. 604, 610 (2000).

Court's scope of review is limited to the administrative record in the first, eighth, and ninth circuits.[47] In all other circuits, the Tax Court can look outside the administrative record.[48] An appeals officer does not abuse their discretion when they fail to consider information that was not provided to them.[49] However, if the taxpayer's circumstances have materially changed since the administrative CDP hearing, the Court has discretion to remand the case for Appeals to consider the new circumstances.[50]

D. Judicial Review Outside the U.S. Tax Court

While caselaw is sparse, courts have addressed I.R.C. § 66(c) in a bankruptcy adversary proceeding[51] and in U.S. district court collection and lien foreclosure actions.[52] Similar considerations described in Chapter 10 also apply here. However, the lack of affirmative judicial review provisions in I.R.C. § 66 may make taxpayers' arguments more difficult.

As with relief under § 6015, community property relief applies to one's personal liability. Thus, in *United States v. Herzog* the district court held (and the Ninth Circuit affirmed) that I.R.C. § 66(c) was irrelevant as a defense to the government's lien foreclosure action, where the government only sought to hold the nonrequesting spouse liable and only sought to collect the nonrequesting spouse's portion of the equity in the property.[53] In contrast, in *United States v. Melot*, where both spouses were liable for tax debt, the district court substantively addressed traditional relief under I.R.C. § 66.[54]

---

[47] Robinette v. Comm'r, 439 F.3d 459 (8th Cir. 2006); Murphy v. Comm'r, 469 F.3d 27, 31 (1st Cir. 2006); Keller v. Comm'r, 568 F.3d 710, 718 (9th Cir. 2009).

[48] Robinette v. Comm'r, 123 T.C. 85 (2004).

[49] Giamelli v. Comm'r, 129 T.C. 107, 115 (2007).

[50] Churchill v. Comm'r, T.C. Memo. 2011-182.

[51] In re Prasch, 1990 WL 169115 (Bankr. E.D. Cal. 1990).

[52] *See, e.g.*, Herzog v. U.S., 201 F.3d 444 (9th Cir. 1999) (unpublished); U.S. v. Melot, 562 Fed. App'x. 646, 654 (10th Cir. 2014).

[53] Herzog v. U.S., 201 F.3d 444 (9th Cir. 1999) (unpublished).

[54] U.S. v. Melot, 562 Fed. App'x. 646, 654 (10th Cir. 2014). Neither the district court nor the circuit court addressed equitable relief as separate from traditional relief. The pro se requesting spouse only asserted relief under § 6015; the district court *sua sponte* considered I.R.C. § 66. *See* U.S. v. Melot, No. CIV. 09-752 JCH/WPL, 2012 WL 1354532 (D. N.M. Mar. 21, 2012).

Chapter 8: Meeting Your Client

I. The First Client Meeting

The first meeting with a client is critical to the success of the client's claim for innocent spouse relief. Asking the right questions at the first meeting may avoid serious problems. For example:

- If a Form 8857 has been filed, how did the client answer certain questions?
- If no Form 8857 was filed, are any deadlines about to expire?
- Has the IRS issued a preliminary determination letter or a final determination letter?
- Has the client filed all returns that were due and paid all taxes since the year(s) at issue?
- Has the IRS begun any collection activities?
- If the client is going through a divorce, are there any tax issues that may bear on the innocent spouse claim?
- Does the client have reason to believe that the nonrequesting spouse may physically threaten them or otherwise retaliate if they file for innocent spouse relief?
- If there is a history of domestic abuse, are there ongoing criminal or civil court cases related to the abuse?

The answers to these and other questions can materially affect the outcome of the client's claim for relief.

Below is a list of actions to be taken and areas of inquiry to be discussed at the first meeting:

1. Complete a Form 2848, Power of Attorney. Err on the side of including more years than may be necessary, and ensure that your authorization continues through at least the current year, if not future years.[1] List both "Income" and "6015 Separation of Liability"[2] as authorized matters.
2. Obtain and review IRS account and wage and income transcripts for the preceding 10 years, and tax return transcripts for the last 4 years.
3. Identify the tax years involved.
4. Ask your client for copies of all relevant income tax returns and copies of correspondence relating to the joint liability.
5. If your client has already filed a Form 8857, obtain a copy of that form and any documents that were attached when it was filed with the IRS.
6. Obtain the name, address, and social security number of the nonrequesting spouse.
7. Identify important timeframes in the case:
    a. Two-year period of limitations: Has the IRS begun any collection activities, such as issuing a Final Notice of Intent to Levy (IRS Letter 1058), or has the IRS offset and applied subsequent year refunds to the years at issue? As noted, if the IRS offset a refund from a later year, the taxpayer has only two years from an offset to file a claim for innocent spouse relief under subsections (b) and (c).[3]
    b. Refunds:[4] Are the time periods for requesting a refund about to expire? Even if no collection action has been initiated, § 6511 governs the time limits for filing a claim for refund.
8. Determine the dates of any separation, divorce, or death of the nonrequesting spouse.

---

[1] Currently, Form 2848 may list up to three future tax years. Always check the instructions for the most current version of the form.

[2] For the separation of liability matter, the corresponding tax form number is "1040 Separate Assessment". When a client first comes to you, the joint account may not have been separated by the IRS. However, it is best practice to list the separated account on Form 2848, in the event the accounts are mirrored during your representation.

[3] *See supra* Chapter 3, I (*First Collection Activity*).

[4] *See infra* Chapter 13, I (*The Refund*).

9. Obtain a copy of any separation agreement or divorce decree to determine whether the nonrequesting spouse has responsibility for the payment of the taxes.
10. Discuss the issue of knowledge with your client:
    a. If this is a deficiency case, what did your client know on the date the return was signed? Did they review the return? If an item was omitted from the return, what did they know about the item?[5]
    b. In an underpayment case, the critical date is also the date the return was signed but the inquiry is different. Did the client have a reasonable belief that the nonrequesting spouse would pay the unpaid tax on the date the return was signed?
11. Analyze your client's financial situation to determine if the facts establish economic hardship. Many low-income clients are living at or below the financial hardship standard.
    a. Advise your client to begin collecting receipts for housing (including utilities and cell phone), transportation (including car note, insurance, gas, repairs, and registration), health care (insurance, co-pays, and prescriptions), and any other major expenses.
    b. To prove income, clients need to provide copies of their most recent tax returns and their most recent paystubs. In addition, if they have a bank account, they should provide you with the three most recent bank statements. Look at the deposits. Deposits can tell a different story than Forms W-2 and Forms 1099.
12. Inquire as to whether there has been physical or mental abuse by the nonrequesting spouse. Ask your client about their access to financial information during the relationship with the nonrequesting spouse. Did the nonrequesting spouse deny the requesting spouse access to financial information in any manner? Who controlled the financial decisions in the home? Did the couple have joint bank accounts? Determine the extent of your client's involvement in the preparation of the income tax returns. Does your client have any accounting or tax education or experience? Was your client allowed to review the income tax returns and to ask questions about items prior to filing?
13. Ascertain whether your client received a significant benefit from the omission of income or a refund. If there was a refund, how were the funds used? Did your client use any part of the refund for other than

---

[5] *See supra* Chapter 3, II (*Duty of Inquiry*).

normal support? Did the couple make any extravagant purchases or go on expensive vacations?

14. Inquire as to whether the client is in compliance with the tax laws. It is important to educate the client about the importance of timely filing and paying taxes while the case is pending and into the future.
15. Discuss any physical or mental health issues your client endured during the years at issue or is currently experiencing. If your client has health issues, it is important to begin acquiring documents that explain those medical conditions and, if possible, the impact the conditions will have on your client's ability to manage financial affairs.

Another practice tip for the client meeting is to discuss the term "innocent spouse." The term may have an upsetting moral connotation for clients, especially if they do not qualify. For example, should a potential client, who has a history of suffering domestic abuse from their spouse, have a joint liability primarily because of income they left off the joint return, then that client will not be able to access § 6015 relief. However, telling them they are not an "innocent spouse" may be confusing and hurtful to the client with such a history. It is therefore important to emphasize that the term refers to specific qualifications under the law that often do not have a direct correlation with who was a "good" or "bad" actor during the marriage in a moral or ethical sense.

II. Reviewing IRS Account Transcripts

If the requesting spouse fails to timely file returns after the joint return at issue, the IRS will argue that the compliance with income tax laws factor should weigh against the requesting spouse. You should therefore use the Power of Attorney to obtain your client's account transcripts from the IRS to review compliance in later years. While the case is pending, it is helpful to contact your client in advance of filing or payment deadlines to remind them to file all returns and pay all taxes due.

III. Documenting Economic Hardship

The revenue procedure allows for a presumption of economic hardship if your client's monthly income is less than 250% of the Federal Poverty Guidelines, unless they have significant assets from which they can draw basic living expenses. If your client qualifies for the presumption then the client will not have to prove his or her monthly basic living expenses.[6] However, if your client is not eligible for the presumption, then the client will have to prove their basic living expenses. If proof is required on the

[6] *See supra* Chapter 6, V (*Proving Economic Hardship*).

economic hardship factor, use IRS Form 433-A (Collection Information Statement) or Form 433-F (a shorter version of the Form 433-A) to prepare a thorough view of the client's financial position.

When preparing these forms, be sure to gather up to date documentation from the client. This includes gathering recent pay records from all sources of employment, bank statements, and receipts of major or ongoing medical expenses.

The Allowable Living Expenses National Standards published each year by the IRS can be used to documents basic living expenses, including food, housekeeping supplies, clothing, and personal care products. Unless your client has a special need, such as more expensive dietary requirements due to a medical condition, it is appropriate to use these standardized numbers and note in the application that you are doing so.

IV. Understanding Related Family Law Matters

If a client is separated from their spouse, the first line of inquiry is whether they have taken any legal action to end the marriage. This requires understanding the basic family law procedures and terms of art in the state where the client lives or has filed. In Alaska, for example, if the parties agree on all issues they can file for a fast-track "dissolution" instead of a "divorce," which is a contested proceeding in that state.[7] A dissolution results in the same outcome as a divorce. Meanwhile, in Massachusetts, regardless of whether the parties agree, only a "divorce" can be filed to end the marriage.[8] Some states, such as Ohio, provide for a "legal separation," in which the parties have a legal agreement dealing with some, but not all, issues of the marriage, and do not actually obtain a divorce.[9] Other states provide a more limited type of proceeding short of divorce called a "separate support" case.[10]

Understanding what the client is doing in state court matters because it determines the precision and accuracy with which the claim for innocent spouse relief can describe the legal status of their marriage and will help explain any related documents relevant to the innocent spouse claim.

Understanding that process can also help the practitioner gather relevant documents from either the client or the family court. A divorce case file can be a valuable trove of critical information that can correlate with several factors in the revenue procedure. A divorce agreement might contain

---

[7] *See* Alaska Stat. § 25.24.200

[8] *See* Mass. Gen. L. c. 208.

[9] *See e.g.*, Oh. Stat. § 3105.171 (containing differences in the division of marital property depending on whether the parties are seeking a divorce or a legal separation.)

[10] *See e.g.*, Mass. Gen. L. § 209 c. 30.

language where the nonrequesting spouse assumes liability for outstanding joint tax debts, which, while not dispositive on its own, will weigh in favor of the spouse seeking innocent spouse relief. The file may also contain detailed information about the family's home life situation, including allegations of abuse, dubious financial dealings, or medical conditions that will speak to the totality of circumstances in the innocent spouse claim. Any findings of fact on such issues by a family court should be strongly considered as evidence in the IRS case. It is therefore important to ask the client for as much detail as possible about the family law case and to seek out the actual file when possible.

V. Documenting Domestic Abuse

The definition of abuse in the revenue procedure is broad. It is not just limited to incidents of physical violence but includes "psychological, sexual, or emotional abuse, including efforts to control, isolate, humiliate, and intimidate the requesting spouse."[11] This is a much larger scope then many state law definitions of abuse which contemplate acts or direct threats of physical violence. When interviewing a client, do not assume that abuse does not apply if they have no history of police involvement or restraining orders against their spouse. It may be that there is long history of control that you can help the client describe through a narrative statement. Adding a written statement signed by the client attesting to such a relationship can preserve those facts for testimony at trial should the case later be taken to the Tax Court.

In situations where there is a history of physical or threatened physical violence, documentary support might be more available. Copies of any restraining orders, criminal case dockets, police or medical reports or any family court history documenting the abuse is key to collect. However, even in cases of serious violence, it is not uncommon to lack documentary evidence. The client's first-person narrative, again in the form of written statements or sworn oral testimony, may still be found credible.

When documenting domestic abuse, do not assume the examiners at the IRS can easily see the pattern being put together. It is important to include as much detail as possible and to explain any documents provided. For example, in some states, restraining orders are primarily issued by police departments while in others they are court orders issued by a judge after a hearing. Explaining exactly what the document is, what it means, and how it was issued can go a long way in connecting the dots for the examiner. The goal is to create an accurate portrait of your client's individual situation.

---

[11] Rev. Proc. 2013-34, 2013-2 C.B. 397 § 4.03(c)(iv).

Chapter 9: Administrative Proceedings

I. Form 8857

In most cases, the election or request for relief begins by filing a Form 8857, Request for Innocent Spouse Relief.[1] Spousal relief claims may be raised at almost any phase of a tax case, including in an examination, in a Tax Court petition for redetermination of a deficiency, and in response to a Collection Due Process notice. Spousal relief can be requested as a collection alternative at any time during the life of the debt.

The following comments may be helpful.

- The IRS has revised Form 8857 several times. It is important that the client fill out the most recent version of Form 8857. Failure to use the most recent form could significantly delay processing of the claim. You can get the most recent Form 8857 at the IRS website.[2]
- The statute of limitations on collection is suspended while the IRS is considering the claim and while the matter is in Tax Court.[3]
- Each taxable year for which relief is being sought must be listed on the Form 8857.

---

[1] A copy of IRS Form 8857 is included at Appendix B, *infra*.

[2] *Forms, Instructions & Publications*, IRS, http://www.irs.gov/forms (last visited Nov. 19, 2021).

[3] I.R.C. § 6015(e)(2).

- If your client is claiming a refund it is important that this request be clearly indicated on the Form 8857.[4]
- It is important that Form 8857 and the attached statements and documents provide as accurate and complete a picture as possible. Self-prepared Forms 8857 often have multiple points of confusion and apparent contradiction, so plan to revise your client's first draft for clarity and completeness.
- Be sure that you have fully investigated the facts and that your client agrees with the scope of the information being disclosed with Form 8857. The IRS will use Form 8857 to attack your client's credibility if her story changes. For example, if your client is reluctant to disclose abuse it is preferable to be vague and leave boxes unchecked, than to check the box "no" in response to that question.[5]
- One of the most important parts of Form 8857 is the request for monthly income and expenses. If the client is living from paycheck to paycheck, collection will prevent them from paying for basic living expenses. It is important to gather documents that prove that collection will create an economic hardship.[6]
- At the end of the Form 8857, the client is asked if there is other information the IRS should consider. We recommend that you assist your client in writing a narrative attachment to supplement the answers provided on the form, giving fuller context and all relevant circumstances.
- When submitting Form 8857, we recommend that you prepare a cover letter or memorandum[7] that explains the facts and analysis establishing your client's eligibility for relief under each applicable subsection of I.R.C. § 6015. Because of the overlap in factors in (b) and (f) cases, the authors' practice is to concentrate the analysis on I.R.C. § 6015(f), and briefly state any claim under § 6015(b).
- In both the client's statement and your memo it is important to discuss all the nonexclusive equitable relief factors, including marital

---

[4] *See infra* Chapter 13 (*Obtaining a Refund from the IRS*).

[5] In *Pullins v. Comm'r*, 136 T.C. 432 (2011), the taxpayer indicated that there was no abuse on Form 8857. When she later testified to abuse, the court did not find her credible. The judge doubted Ms. Pullins's explanation that she checked the wrong box, pointing out that the instructions ask for corroborating information and documents, and Ms. Pullins had provided none with her Form 8857.

[6] Rev. Proc. 2013-34 contains guidelines for proving economic hardship. Some low-income taxpayers benefit from a presumption that collection would create an economic hardship and will not have to prove their basic living expenses. *See supra* Chapter 6, V (*Proving Economic Hardship*).

[7] The authors' practice is to incorporate the legal memorandum into the cover letter accompanying Form 8857 and the supporting documents.

status, economic hardship, knowledge, health issues, compliance with the law, and significant benefit. Even if you are requesting relief under I.R.C. § 6015(b) or (c), the IRS may review the claim under I.R.C. § 6015(f) as well, so providing information responsive to the factors set forth in Revenue Procedure 2013-34 is always helpful.

As part of the memorandum, it is helpful to include the following table showing how you believe the seven factors should be allocated to the requesting spouse, to the IRS, or to the neutral category.

Revenue Procedure 2013-34 Table

Factors	Factor Favors Relief	Factor Favors Liability	Factor is Neutral
1. Marital Status			
2. Economic Hardship			
3. Knowledge			
4. Compliance with Tax Laws			
5. Legal Obligation to Pay			
6. Significant Benefit			
7. Mental or Physical Health			

II. Cincinnati Centralized Innocent Spouse Operation—Covington, Kentucky

Almost all administrative claims for innocent spouse relief are initiated by submitting Form 8857 to the Cincinnati Centralized Innocent Spouse Operation ("CCISO"). The form and accompanying documents can be faxed to the IRS at 855-233-8558 or mailed via U.S.P.S. to the following address:

Internal Revenue Service
P.O. Box 120053
Covington, KY 41012

If using a private delivery service, the address is:

Internal Revenue Service
7940 Kentucky Drive, Stop 840F
Florence, KY 41042

If mailing Form 8857, it is good practice to use certified, registered, or express mail to establish a mailing date and confirm delivery. Likewise, if faxing, keep the fax confirmation sheet. Occasionally, the IRS cannot locate the Form 8857 that was received. The certified mail documents then become of great value, to establish the timeliness of a refund claim or to establish Tax Court jurisdiction under I.R.C. § 6015(e)(1)(A)(i)(II). The phone number for the Centralized Innocent Spouse Operation is 855-851-2009.[8]

If you are already working with an examination, appeals, or collection employee, you should ask the employee where the claim for innocent spouse relief should be filed. Some employees prefer that you mail the original Form 8857 to the centralized group in Covington and simply provide a copy to the employee for their files. In other cases, the IRS employee may instruct you file the original Form 8857 with them.

III. Telling the Story

Winning your client's case is all about telling a credible and persuasive story. When your client submits a Form 8857, it becomes one of many thousands of innocent spouse relief claims filed annually.[9] The claim is assigned to an examiner, who makes a good faith effort to review the claim. It is important to do more than file a Form 8857. It is important to tell a compelling story.

Consider the following. Taxpayer A and Taxpayer B have essentially the same facts and circumstances. They are divorced working women, who are raising two minor children. Both were in abusive marriages and are now earning about $15,000 annually cleaning hotel rooms. Their former spouses were self-employed truck drivers who did not pay estimated taxes. They both claimed the earned income tax credit in subsequent years and the IRS offset their last two refunds and applied it to the joint tax debts.

Taxpayer A prepares Form 8857 and answers each question accurately, but does not explain the nature and extent of the abuse or provide any documents. In filling out her monthly income and expenses, she does not include any supporting financial documents because none were currently available.

Taxpayer B prepares Form 8857 and answers each question accurately and submits as an attachment a narrative that discusses all of the factors set forth in Revenue Procedure 2013-34. She explains how her husband physically attacked her when she asked a question about how the taxes would be paid. She also provides a police report that was issued on the day the return was signed and describes the attack by the nonrequesting

---

[8] *See* Location for Taxpayer to File Form 8857, I.R.M. 25.15.2.3 (09-08-2020).

[9] In fiscal year 2015, CCISO received about 47,400 requests for relief. National Taxpayer Advocate 2017 Objectives Report to Congress Vol. I, 177 (2016).

spouse, and an order of protection signed by a domestic relations judge. In support of her claim of economic hardship, Taxpayer B includes documents demonstrating that if collection continues, she will not be able to pay her rent and basic living expenses. Finally, she describes how her husband filed returns with balances due in past years but always paid the tax due in a few months.

It is pretty easy to see why Taxpayer B's claim for innocent spouse relief is more likely to be approved. The IRS employee assigned to these claims has a significant inventory to review and deadlines to meet. When a claim arrives that tells a compelling story and provides back-up documents, the claim can be processed and approved in a reasonable time. On the other hand, if the Form 8857 fails to convince the employee that relief is warranted, the employee may simply deny the claim rather than take the time to request additional information.

IV. CCISO Review[10]

The IRS begins its review by checking for processability of the Form 8857. (E.g. is the form signed under penalty of perjury? Is there a joint liability?) Next, the submission is screened for allegations indicating that the joint return may be invalid. If such allegations are present, they are resolved before spousal relief is considered.

If the request meets threshold processability and eligibility criteria, and the joint return is valid, the CCISO employee will research the accounts of both spouses and investigate the claim using databases and research tools available to the IRS. CCISO will also mail a letter and a questionnaire (Form 12508) to the nonrequesting spouse.[11]

While the nonrequesting spouse is entitled to notice of the claim and may participate in the process, the nonrequesting spouse will not automatically be sent a copy of the Form 8857 or accompanying documents. The IRS will not contact witnesses or third parties, as it is constrained by the disclosure provisions of I.R.C. § 6103.

V. Speaking with the CCISO Employee

IRS employees in the Centralized Innocent Spouse operation may call the requesting spouse (or representative) to request clarification or additional information before making a preliminary determination.[12] Supplemental information and documents may be faxed to CCISO.

---

[10] *See generally* Innocent Spouse Relief Processing Procedures, I.R.M. 25.15.18 (01-15-2020); Administrative Processes, I.R.M. 25.15.1.3 (04-02-2020).

[11] Treas. Reg. § 51.6015-6(a)(1).

[12] No Replies, I.R.M. 25.15.18.5.2.10 (02-06-2017).

If you know in advance that your client wishes to provide sensitive information over the phone rather than in writing, this opportunity should be requested with Form 8857. Because of the importance of building the administrative record for potential court review, it is best to provide a sworn statement or documents whenever they are available, unless your client has significant safety concerns.

A phone call with CCISO to provide information is informal, and the call is not recorded or transcribed. The process is similar to a call with an IRS Appeals Officer. The IRS employee may have questions for your client and should also give your client the opportunity to add information. All conversations should be memorialized in a follow-up letter to the IRS employee shortly after the call. The letter should be as detailed as possible within the limits of any safety concerns. This is crucial to make an accurate record for appeal.

VI. The Preliminary Determination Letter

After the employee has contacted the nonrequesting spouse and completed their review of the Form 8857 and other information submitted, the examiner will issue a preliminary determination letter.[13] In the preliminary determination letter the IRS will propose to grant some, all, or none of the relief requested. It will also indicate whether your client will get a refund. The preliminary determination letter is not required by statute. It offers both spouses the opportunity to request review of the IRS's proposed decision by the Independent Office of Appeals. If the IRS proposes to grant full relief, this is the nonrequesting spouse's only opportunity to appeal that decision. The nonrequesting spouse cannot petition for Tax Court review.[14]

If neither spouse requests Appeals review within the time provided in the preliminary determination letter, the IRS will issue a final determination letter, notifying the requesting spouse of the right to file a petition in the Tax Court.

VII. The IRS Independent Office of Appeals

The preliminary determination gives both the requesting spouse and the nonrequesting spouse the opportunity for review by the IRS Independent Office of Appeals.[15] An Appeals conference is very similar to having a call with a CCISO employee, and the same cautionary tips about the administrative record apply.

---

[13] Administrative Processes, I.R.M. 25.15.1.3 (04-02-2020).

[14] Maier v. Comm'r, 119 T.C. 267 (2002), *aff'd*, 360 F.3d 361 (2d Cir. 2004).

[15] For information about the appeals process, *see* IRS Publication 5, Your Appeal Rights and How to Prepare a Protest if You Disagree, available at irs.gov/forms.

In considering whether a requesting spouse should seek review by Appeals at this time, the representative should consider a number of matters:

- Are the facts compelling? If the facts make out a strong case for relief, it may be advantageous to request an Appeals hearing. Cases can often be settled at the Appeals level.
- Is the administrative record complete, or are there additional documents you could supply at the Appeals level? Remember that the Tax Court's review is generally limited to the administrative record. An administrative appeal prior to the IRS's Final Determination is an opportunity to expand the record.
- Did the nonrequesting spouse submit a questionnaire or otherwise participate at the administrative level? An administrative appeal provides an opportunity to review and rebut any evidence provided by the other spouse. Also, a nonrequesting spouse cannot prevent a settlement at the administrative level between the IRS and the requesting spouse, whereas they can prevent settlement in Tax Court.[16]
- In an appeal you will have the right to see the administrative record,[17] including the IRS employee's notes regarding their research and conclusions. If the explanation in the preliminary determination letter is cursory, reviewing the record before CCISO may give you insight into why the request was denied, and help you prepare for a successful Tax Court appeal.
- Does the client have confidentiality or safety concerns regarding a court appeal?
- How much time has passed since the Form 8857 was received? If more than six months have passed, the requesting spouse has a statutory right to file a petition in Tax Court for a review of her claim.[18] It is not necessary to wait for the final determination letter. On the other hand, if your client's circumstances have changed in favorable ways since the Form 8857 was submitted, you may want to seek Appeals review in order to update the record.
- Does your client have an urgent need for their refund? If your client is experiencing an economic hardship and will receive a refund if relief is granted, it may be faster to proceed straight to Tax Court.

---

[16] *See infra* Chapter 11, VIII (*Dealing with Intervenors*).
[17] I.R.C. § 7803(e)(7).
[18] I.R.C. § 6501(e).

- Do you wish to pursue attorneys' fees and costs? If so, you must exhaust administrative appeals.[19]

VIII. The Final Determination

The final determination letter concludes the administrative proceedings and informs the taxpayer of the IRS determination granting or denying relief. Like a notice of deficiency, the final determination letter is a jurisdictional "ticket" to the Tax Court.[20] Importantly, the record for judicial review is generally closed at the time of the determination.

---

[19] *See infra* Chapter 11, IV (*Laying the Groundwork for Attorneys' Fees Under Section 7430: Qualified Offers*).

[20] I.R.C. § 6015(e)(1)(A).

Chapter 10: Judicial Fora

I. Jurisdiction in the United States Tax Court

The vast majority of innocent spouse cases are litigated in the Tax Court.

As of January 2021, the Court consisted of seventeen judges, ten senior judges, and six special trial judges.[1] Although located in Washington, D.C., the Tax Court is a traveling court. Judges travel to specially designated cities and generally hold trial calendars for one week. During that week, the judge will hear a number of cases.

The Tax Court acquires jurisdiction in innocent spouse cases in one of three ways. In a traditional notice of deficiency case, a taxpayer can raise the issue of innocent spouse relief as an affirmative defense.[2] A second jurisdictional basis exists in collection due process cases under I.R.C. §§ 6320 and 6330. I.R.C. § 6330(c)(2) expressly allows a taxpayer to raise "appropriate spousal defenses."

The third method is standalone judicial review under I.R.C. § 6015(e). I.R.C. § 6015(e) provides the Tax Court with jurisdiction to consider the denial of a claim for innocent spouse relief. Unlike a deficiency proceeding

---

[1] "United States Tax Court: Judges," *available at* www.ustaxcourt.gov/judges.html (last accessed January 21, 2021).

[2] *See* Corson v. Comm'r, 114 T.C. 354 (2000) (explaining that the Tax Court has jurisdiction to review a claim for relief from joint and several liability when such a claim is raised as an affirmative defense in a petition for redetermination of a deficiency filed pursuant to § 6213(a)).

or a collection due process proceeding, the issues are restricted to relief from joint liability.

Cases that proceed to court after the filing of a Form 8857 and a petition from a final determination letter are known as "standalone" cases. In a standalone proceeding, the nonrequesting spouse is entitled to notice and the right to intervene.[3]

Section 6015(e) provides taxpayers with two opportunities to petition the Tax Court: (1) within 90 days of the date a final determination letter is issued, a taxpayer may file a petition for review of the IRS determination pursuant to § 6015(e)(1)(A)(i)(1); and (2) six months after filing an election or request for innocent spouse relief with the IRS, if the IRS has not resolved the claim, pursuant to I.R.C. § 6015(e)(A)(i)(II).

It is crucial to understand that the 90-day deadline to file a petition for innocent spouse relief in the Tax Court after the Final Notice of Determination is considered jurisdictional by the Court. That means that failure to postmark, or electronically file, the petition by that deadline will result in the taxpayer losing their right to bring the claim in the Court because the allowed 90-day period itself is what grants the Court jurisdiction to hear the case. Under this interpretation, there is no room to argue that there is a reasonable excuse that allows for equitable tolling of the deadline. To date, three circuit courts have affirmed this interpretation by the Tax Court.[4]

II. United States District Courts and Court of Federal Claims

The two contexts where § 6015 may be relevant in United States District Court proceedings are in lien foreclosure cases brought by the United States Government for the IRS under § 7403 and refund suits brought by the taxpayer under § 1346 (which may also be brought in the United States Court of Federal Claims).

A. Lien Foreclosure

If the Government brings a suit to foreclose a lien on real property owned by joint taxpayers, it may be possible to use § 6015 as an avenue to help one spouse at least recuperate some of the proceeds of the foreclosure. While there is no binding precedent saying that § 6015 cannot be a defense to foreclosure, the prevailing legal theory is that it cannot stop a foreclosure. This is because a lien foreclosure is an *in rem* proceeding against the property, while winning a § 6015 claim absolves personal liability but

---

[3] King v. Comm'r, 115 T.C. 118 (2000).

[4] *See* Matuzak v. Comm'r, 862 F.3d 192 (2d Cir. 2017); Rubel v. Comm'r, 856 F.3d 301 (3d Cir. 2017); Nauflett v. Comm'r, 892 F.3d 649 (4th Cir. 2018).

does not evaporate *in rem* jurisdiction over the property if the co-owner also maintains a liability.[5]

However, if a taxpayer is facing a lien foreclosure for a joint tax debt, and they have a strong case that they are entitled to § 6015 relief, then it may be a worthwhile strategy to file a motion to stay the foreclosure proceedings pending the outcome of an innocent spouse case. In this scenario, the taxpayer would file a Form 8857 with the IRS and, depending on the outcome, later petition the U.S. Tax Court, while the District Court foreclosure case remained stayed.[6] A version of this approach may be to reach an agreement with the Government in the District Court for the foreclosure to move forward while asking the Court to hold the potentially non-liable spouse's share in escrow pending the resolution of the § 6015 proceedings.

If successful in the parallel § 6015 proceeding, then the taxpayer could argue in the District Court that they are entitled to their half of the proceedings resulting from a foreclosure sale. Alternatively, it may be possible to block the actual foreclosure, after winning innocent spouse status, not on personal liability grounds, but by arguing that certain equitable factors, the so-called *Rogers* factors, make it inappropriate to foreclose when there is a non-delinquent co-owner of the property.[7] These factors require a high bar to meet.

B. Refund Suits

It remains an open question as to whether § 6015 claims can form the basis for a refund suit in the United States District Courts or the Federal Court of Claims. 28 U.S.C. § 1346(a) conveys jurisdiction on those courts to hear suits in which taxpayers allege that tax was "wrongfully collected" or "excessive." Meanwhile, I.R.C. § 7422 requires that a taxpayer first make an application for a refund to the Secretary, and thus exhaust their administrative remedies before they can file a complaint in the U.S. District Court or Court of Federal Claims. Only once a taxpayer has received a final denial from the IRS, or when 6 months have passed since filing their

---

[5] *See* U.S. v. Kraus, No. 3:16-cv-5449 (W.D. Wash. April 3, 2018).

[6] The strategy has prevailed in some district courts but not in others. *See* U.S. v. LeBeau, No. 3:17-cv-01046 (S.D. Cal. Oct. 16, 2018); *but see* U.S. v. Drew, 670 Fed.Appx. 170 (4th Cir. 2016).

[7] U.S. v. Rogers, 461 U.S. 677, 709–11 (1983) (The factors to balance when deciding whether to authorize a foreclosure sale under § 7403 when the interests of nondelinquent third parties are involved, are the following: (1) "the extent to which the Government's financial interests would be prejudiced if it were relegated to a forced sale of the partial interest actually liable for the delinquent taxes;" (2) "whether the third party with a nonliable separate interest in the property would, in the normal course of events, have a legally recognized expectation that such separate property would not be subject to forced sale by the delinquent taxpayer or his or her creditors;" (3) "the likely prejudice to the third party, both in personal dislocation costs and in practical under compensation;" and (4) "the relative character and value of the nonliable and liable interests held in the property.").

claim without a determination, may they file their complaint in these fora.[8] It is also established Supreme Court case law that the taxpayer must have first paid the disputed tax liability in full before they can seek a refund in those courts.[9] This jurisdictional bar is known as the *Flora* rule.

The *Flora* rule is an immediate disadvantage for many taxpayers seeking innocent spouse relief. However, there are circumstances where even low-income taxpayers may satisfy it. For example, if a taxpayer has had several years of large refunds offset against the liability for the joint tax year or years in question, then they might find themselves with a fully paid liability. In these circumstances, each separate payment will be subject to the time rules governing refunds. Each administrative claim for refund, including through the use of Form 8857, must be made within the bounds of I.R.C. § 6511 and then each of those claims will, in turn, be subject to the time rules for filing the court action for refund. A taxpayer who has paid off a liability over many years may therefore find themself only able to recoup the most recent payments when they finally qualify to bring a case under the *Flora* rule.

Once the *Flora* rule is satisfied, a taxpayer must overcome the hurdle as to whether § 6015 can be a basis for a refund under § 7422. Currently, there is limited case law on this issue and many district courts have rejected these suits.[10] In 2018, however, the U.S. District of Oregon issued an opinion finding that such suits should be allowed under § 7422. The Court reasoned that the premise of an innocent spouse claim, in which it would be inequitable to hold the taxpayer liable for the tax due on a joint return, falls within the plain meaning of a "wrongfully collected" tax.[11]

III. United States Bankruptcy Courts

As with U.S. District Court jurisdiction, there is dispute as to whether the U.S. Bankruptcy Courts have jurisdiction to hear innocent spouse cases. Under § 505a of the United States Bankruptcy Code ("Bankruptcy Code"), the court has the power to "determine the amount or legality of any tax, any fine or penalty relating to a tax, or any addition to tax, whether or not previously assessed, whether or not paid and whether or not contested before and adjudicated by a judicial or administrative tribunal of competent jurisdiction."[12]

---

[8] 26 U.S.C. § 6532(a).

[9] Flora v. United States, 362 U.S. 145 (1960).

[10] *See, e.g.*, Chandler v. United States, 338 F. Supp. 3d.592 (N.D. Tex 2018).

[11] Hockin v. United States, 400 F. Supp. 3d 1085 (D. Or. 2019).

[12] 11 U.S.C. § 505(a).

Most bankruptcy courts have historically interpreted this provision as excluding jurisdiction to hear innocent spouse claims for equitable relief. Shortly after § 6015(f) was added to the Internal Revenue Code in 1998, some bankruptcy opinions interpreted § 6015 as excluding judicial review.[13] Meanwhile, other courts did proceed to determine the merits of claims based on § 6015(b) or (c) relief within the bankruptcy case.[14]

While the issue may still be unsettled, at least two bankruptcy courts have issued orders declaring that bankruptcy courts do have jurisdiction over § 6015(f) cases. In 2017, the Bankruptcy Court for the Southern District of Texas, in the case *In re Pendergraf*, denied an IRS motion to dismiss a debtor's adversary proceeding to determine the validity of an IRS lien on her home in which she raised § 6015(f) as a defense.[15] The Court acknowledged that § 6015(f) only confers jurisdiction on the IRS to review an original claim for relief. However, it reasoned that because § 6015(e)(1)(A) allows the Tax Court to review a claim once denied by the IRS, the Bankruptcy Court may also review the claim through the Court's power to determine tax liability under Bankruptcy Code § 505(a). Because § 505(a) grants the Court power to determine the validity of tax liabilities and penalties, it is another "remedy provided by law" under § 6015(e)(1)(A). The *Pendergraf* Court further noted that it could exercise jurisdiction because, in that case, the determination of innocent spouse liability was directly tied to the administration of the bankruptcy estate because of the adversary proceeding involving the validity of a tax lien.

In 2021, the Bankruptcy Court for the Eastern District of Louisiana adopted the language and logic of *In re Pendergraf* when denying a debtor's motion for summary judgment. The debtor had raised an innocent spouse claim to challenge the IRS's proof of claim in the bankruptcy case.[16] The Court, though disagreeing that the debtor had met her burden in her summary judgment motion, agreed that it had jurisdiction to hear her claim as a core proceeding under Bankruptcy Code § 157 and under its § 505(a) authority. It noted, however, that in using innocent spouse to challenge a proof of claim, the burden is on the debtor to prove that she meets all the required elements of innocent spouse relief.

These two cases suggest that it is possible to raise innocent spouse relief under § 6015(f) in bankruptcy proceedings if a Form 8857 has already

---

[13] *See* In re French, 255 B.R. 1, 2 (Bankr. N.D. Ohio 2000) ("Accordingly, as § 6015(f) specifically provides that only the 'Secretary' may determine a taxpayer's entitlement to relief under that section, this Court finds that it has no jurisdictional authority to hear the Plaintiff's case.").

[14] *See, e.g.*, In re Hinckley, 256 B.R. 814 (Bankr. M.D. Fla. 2000); In re Shafman, 267 B.R. 709 (N.D. W. Va. 2001).

[15] In re Pendergraf, WL1091935 (Bankr. S.D. Tex. 2017).

[16] In re Bowman, WL2523498 (E.D. La. 2021).

been denied by the IRS and if determining innocent spouse relief is integral to determining the validity of tax liabilities in the bankruptcy estate.

Chapter 11: The Tax Court—Pretrial

I. The Petition

Beginning a Tax Court case is relatively easy. The pleadings can be far less complex than pleadings filed in refund cases in federal district court. The requirements are set out at Tax Court Rule 34.[1]

A Tax Court case begins with the filing of a petition. The only documents attached to the petition should be a copy of the IRS notice providing the Court with jurisdiction (the "ticket to Tax Court"),[2] a Statement of Taxpayer Identification Number, a Request for Place of Trial, and the filing fee or waiver request form. If you attach other documents to the petition, the Tax Court will return the documents. You will have an opportunity

---

[1] *See also* Tax Ct. R. 321 (commencement of standalone spousal relief cases), 331 (commencement of collection due process cases). A copy of the court's simplified petition form is included at Appendix D, *infra*. The Tax Court has established rules on redacting social security numbers and other sensitive information in filings. *See* Tax Ct. R. 27 (Privacy Protection For Filings Made With The Court).

It is imperative for representatives to read the applicable Tax Court rules in full. They are posted on the Court's website, www.ustaxcourt.gov. For an in-depth discussion of Tax Court procedure, *see* Chapter 7 of Effectively Representing Your Client Before the IRS (ABA 8th Ed. 2021). The chapter is available as a standalone book: Sean Murphy Akins, Kandyce Lyndsey Korotky, and David M. Sams, Litigating a Case in Tax Court (ABA 2021).

[2] This ticket will usually be a final Notice of Determination or a Statutory Notice of Deficiency. Of course, a final determination letter may not be available if the taxpayer is relying on the six-month time period in I.R.C. § 6015(e)(1)(A)(i)(II).

to present documents and additional information when you meet with counsel for the IRS. And, of course, you will be able to introduce evidence at the trial, subject to the limits of the administrative record rule.

Tax Court petitioners can elect small case procedures if the amount of relief sought is less than $50,000.[3] If no election is made on the petition, the case will proceed under regular procedures. Small case procedures have advantages and disadvantages. More places of trial are available in small cases, and the rules of evidence are slightly relaxed. Post-trial briefs are not required, which makes small cases less time-consuming and expensive to litigate. The main disadvantage of small case procedures is that no appeal can be taken from the Tax Court's decision.[4]

At the time that the petition is filed, the taxpayer must file a Request for Place of Trial, designating the city in which the case should be tried. The Tax Court provides a list of choices for location of the trial. There is no way to identify in advance which judge will hear the case, although some judges tend to cover certain trial locations.

Also at the time a petition is filed, a filing fee or a request for waiver of the fee must be submitted. The current filing fee in the Tax Court is $60. To obtain a fee waiver, the taxpayer must complete and file an Application for Waiver of Tax Court Filing Fee and Affidavit, which is available on the Tax Court website.

II. Discovery

A. Informal and Formal Discovery

Discovery may be more important in an innocent spouse case than in other Tax Court cases. In some cases, the IRS disallows equitable relief with a final determination letter that runs through the factors in a cursory manner and fails to adequately inform the taxpayer what is in dispute. Discovery can and should be used to define and narrow the issues for trial. Discovery also allows a representative to conserve his or her resources.[5]

It is important to understand how discovery works in the Tax Court. The Tax Court requires the parties to informally exchange information before initiating formal discovery (interrogatories, requests for documents, and

---

[3] *See* I.R.C. § 7463; Tax Ct. R. 170-174, 321(c).

[4] I.R.C. § 7463(b).

[5] Tax Court judges expect the parties to reach agreement on issues that are not in dispute. If the IRS does not contest knowledge in an I.R.C. § 6015(b) case, the court does not want to hear proof on the issue since it is not in dispute. A good way to irritate the court is for the parties (the taxpayer and the IRS) to arrive at calendar call and announce that there are ten issues for trial in a case when there are really only two or three disputed issues. The best practice is to file a Stipulation of Settled Issues before trial.

requests for admissions).[6] Therefore, it is necessary to send a letter, often called a "Branerton" letter, to IRS counsel informally requesting information and documents. You should set a reasonable response date, for example three weeks, for the IRS to respond, and follow up at least once by phone or email. If IRS counsel fails to respond, then you can begin formal discovery.[7] Discovery must be completed more than 45 days before the first day of the Tax Court trial session or there will not be sufficient time to file any motions to compel any failure by the IRS to comply.[8]

B. Helpful Discovery in Spousal Relief Cases

What types of discovery might be effective in an innocent spouse case? Of course, you would want different information depending on which subsection of § 6015 was at issue, but let's consider an equitable relief case. It is in your client's best interests to ask the IRS to identify which factors it agrees are in your client's favor and which factors are not. You also need to know if other facts and circumstances beyond the listed factors were considered by the IRS. If you do not make the request, you will have to prove all seven factors and you may not be adequately prepared to address other facts the IRS views as important. On the other hand, if the IRS responds that the marital status and knowledge are in your client's favor, then you know that you have eliminated those issues and can focus on establishing the other factors, such as economic hardship and significant benefit. Agreeing to matters which are not disputed conserves resources by reducing trial preparation.

Once the IRS identifies the factors it believes are not favorable, you can ask what facts the IRS relied on in reaching a determination that the factor was not favorable. This is very important. For example, if the IRS determines that economic hardship was not a factor in your client's favor and in providing its analysis, demonstrates that it did not fully consider all the taxpayer's basic living expenses, you have learned a lot. You can ask the IRS attorney why they did not include health care expenses or why they omitted the monthly car payment. You may be able to persuade the IRS attorney to concede this factor prior to trial and if they do not change their position, you can ask them to stipulate to the supporting documents such as receipts or loan statements. You should go through this drill for each factor that the IRS says is not in your client's favor.

---

[6] *See* Branerton Co. v. Comm'r, 61 T.C. 691 (1974); Tax Ct. R. 70; Schneider Ints., L.P. v. Comm'r, 119 T.C. 151 (2002).

[7] Adams v. Comm'r, 520 F. App'x 934 (11th Cir. 2013). Carefully review the Tax Court rules; some types of discovery require court approval. *See generally* Tax Ct. R. Titles VII through X.

[8] Tax Ct. R. 70(a)(2).

Consider also whether you need to serve a subpoena on third parties for documents or testimony regarding the case.[9] There is no subpoena power at the administrative level, so the Tax Court proceeding is your client's first opportunity to issue third party subpoenas. Unlike in federal district court, in the Tax Court a subpoena to produce documents must be returnable at a hearing or trial session.[10] You must either issue a subpoena returnable at the calendar call or (preferably) file a Motion for Document Subpoena hearing. The Court will generally set a hearing approximately two weeks prior to the calendar call.[11]

III. Addressing the Record Rule

For petitions filed after July 1, 2019, the Tax Court's review (at least in standalone cases) is limited to "the administrative record established at the time of the determination" plus "any additional newly discovered or previously unavailable evidence."[12] Section 6015 does not define the administrative record, and the IRS has suggested in court filings that it should be defined as in CDP cases, as set out in Treasury Regulation § 301.6330-1(f)(2).[13]

The Tax Court has not yet fleshed out the parameters of its new scope of review, which presents many opportunities for advocacy. For example, the limitations of the IRS's administrative process may impact the court's view of "previously unavailable" evidence. In *Fatty v. Commissioner*, the Court allowed both spouses to testify at trial and treated their testimony as newly available evidence because the taxpayer was not able to give sworn testimony in the administrative phase of the case, and neither he nor his wife were subject to cross-examination.[14]

As of this writing, other unresolved questions resulting from the statute change include:

---

[9] Tax Ct. R. 148.

[10] I.R.C. § 7456(a).

[11] *See* U.S. Tax Court, Subpoenas for Remote Proceedings, https://www.ustaxcourt.gov/resources/zoomgov/subpoenas_for_remote_proceedings.pdf [https://perma.cc/76BL-78GT] (revised Dec. 10, 2020). While this guidance was developed for remote proceedings, litigants on track for an in-person trial can also request a remote document subpoena hearing.

[12] I.R.C. § 6015(e)(7); Sutherland v. Comm'r, 155 T.C. No. 6 (2020).

[13] *See* Grady v. Comm'r, Docket No. 016411-17S, Brief for Respondent (Oct. 2019). *See also* Christine Speidel, *Taxpayer First Act Update: Innocent Spouse Tangles Begin*, Procedurally Taxing (Oct. 10, 2019), https://procedurallytaxing.com/taxpayer-first-act-update-innocent-spouse-tangles-begin/ [https://perma.cc/3K6F-2MZ4].

[14] Fatty v. Comm'r, No. 3787-20S, 2021 WL 1720004 (U.S. Tax Court Bench Op. Mar. 16, 2021) (nonprecedential). The Court specifically noted the nonprecedential nature of the case in its opinion. Practitioners should be prepared to advocate for this approach in other cases.

- Whether the record rule applies if there is no Final Determination letter when the petition is filed;
- Whether the Tax Court might now have the authority to remand cases to the IRS for further development;[15] and
- Whether any judicially-recognized exceptions to the record rule apply in this context.[16]

Any disputes relating to the court's scope of review or admissible evidence at trial should be identified and fleshed out in pretrial discovery. Identifying disputes about the scope of the record early on will allow you to strategize and potentially resolve the disputes through a pretrial motion.

Tax Court judges generally welcome requests for a pretrial conference call with the parties. At the conference call, it is a good idea to bring any disputed issues to the judge's attention and inquire whether the judge would prefer to receive a motion, or to have the issue addressed in the parties' pretrial memoranda.

Some judges have proactively issued an order before trial asking the parties to agree on the administrative record and discuss the scope of evidence admissible at trial under I.R.C. § 6015(e)(7). If your judge does not issue such an order, but you believe these issues are disputed, ask for a conference call with the judge to determine the best way to raise (and hopefully resolve) these issues before trial. Particularly where the government seeks to restrict your client's testimony, consider filing a motion in limine asking the court to resolve any disputes about permissible areas of testimony ahead of trial.

IV. Laying the Groundwork for Attorneys' Fees Under Section 7430

A. Background

Taxpayers can recover attorney fees in tax cases in two manners. Traditionally, taxpayers could recover reasonable litigation costs only if they were the prevailing party and could prove that the IRS position was not substantially justified. This is a difficult standard to meet. By far the better tactic to recover litigation costs is to make a "qualified offer."

If a qualified offer is made and later a court rules that the taxpayer owes an amount equal to or less than the amount of the offer, the taxpayer can

---

[15] *See* Carlton Smith, *Should the Tax Court Allow Remands in Light of the Taxpayer First Act Innocent Spouse Provisions?*, Procedurally Taxing (Oct. 17, 2019), https://procedurallytaxing.com/should-the-tax-court-allow-remands-in-light-of-the-taxpayer-first-act-innocent-spouse-provisions/ [https://perma.cc/4YAW-8PV6].

[16] *See* Kasper v. Comm'r, 150 T.C. No. 2 (2018) (*citing* Esch v. Yeutter, 876 F.2d 976, 991 (D.C. Cir. 1989)).

recover attorney fees without regard to whether the IRS position was substantially justified. Removing the requirement to prove substantial justification is a valuable change over the traditional method for recovering fees.

B. *Traditional Attorney Fees Under Section 7430*

Section 7430 authorizes reasonable litigation costs paid or incurred in a court proceeding brought by or against the United States in connection with the determination, collection or refund of any tax. The taxpayer must establish the following:

- He or she is the prevailing party.
- He or she has exhausted administrative remedies.
- He or she has not unreasonably protracted the court proceedings; and
- The litigation costs are reasonable.

Generally, a taxpayer is considered the prevailing party if the taxpayer substantially prevailed and the Commissioner's position is not substantially justified. The Commissioner's position is substantially justified if based upon all the facts and circumstances and legal precedents, the Commissioner acted reasonably.[17]

No action is required prior to receipt of the court's opinion to claim attorney fees under the traditional method. After the court issues its opinion, the attorney files their motion for reasonable litigation costs.

C. *Qualified Offers*

Qualified offers present a very different landscape, because the taxpayer must affirmatively make an offer at least 30 days before trial,[18] and if the taxpayer does better than the offer at trial they do not have to prove that the IRS position was not substantially justified to be considered the prevailing party.[19] The other requirements listed above still apply.

Making a qualified offer often promotes an early settlement of the case. Though you cannot recover fees if the qualified offer is accepted, resolving the case by settlement saves valuable resources.[20]

Here are the requirements for a qualified offer:

- The offer must be in writing.

---

[17] Pierce v. Underwood, 487 U.S. 552 (1988). The taxpayer must also meet net worth limits under I.R.C. § 7430(c)(4)(A)(ii).

[18] *See* I.R.C. § 7430(g)(2) (defining the qualifying offer period).

[19] I.R.C. § 7430(c)(4)(E).

[20] Though you cannot recover litigation fees under the qualified offer provisions if a settlement is reached, taxpayers can still request traditional litigation fees under section 7430(a), but they must prove the IRS position was not substantially justified.

- The offer must say it is a qualified offer for purposes of I.R.C. § 7430.
- The offer must specify the amount of money being offered without regard to interest.
- The offer must be made during the qualified offer period.
- The offer remains open until the earlier of 1) the date the IRS rejects the offer; 2) the date the trial begins; or 3) the 90th day after the date of the offer.

Qualified offers are especially useful in innocent spouse cases, because the judicial decisions usually are entirely for one party or the other party. Here is an example of how a qualified offer would work in an innocent spouse case.

Taxpayer A filed a Form 8857 in January 2020 in an underpayment case seeking relief from joint liabilities for 2015 and 2016. In May 2020, the IRS issued a preliminary determination denying relief under § 6015(f). At that time, the taxpayer engaged an attorney. The attorney determined that the client had a good equitable relief case but had not provided essential information. In late May 2020, the attorney requested an Appeals conference and sent additional information, including the following: 1) specific information relating to the requesting spouse's economic hardship; 2) specific information regarding physical abuse including an order of protection and judicial papers showing that the nonrequesting spouse was convicted of domestic violence; and 3) an affidavit from the client showing how the nonrequesting spouse controlled the household finances and the return preparation. The Appeals Officer eventually issued a final determination letter denying relief, and the taxpayer petitioned the Tax Court in December 2020.

In January 2021, the attorney sent a qualified offer proposing to settle all of the issues for a payment of $100. The IRS had 90 days from the date of the qualified offer to consider the offer.

If the case was tried and the Tax Court ruled that the client was entitled to innocent spouse relief for both years, the client could then request litigation costs from the date of the qualified offer. Whether the IRS position was substantially justified would not be a part of the court's determination of whether fees were allowable. The only reviewable issues would be whether the client made a timely qualified offer and whether the court's decision was equal to or less than the qualified offer.[21]

Qualified offers can be a useful tool to get IRS Counsel's attention and demonstrate your belief in the strength of your case. However, do not count

[21] *See* Estate of Lippitz v. Comm'r, T.C. Memo. 2007-293.

on actually getting paid. The IRS will often concede a case well past the 90-day offer period, sometimes on the eve of trial, and then assert that fees are not available because the court's decision is pursuant to a settlement rather than a contested trial.[22]

V. The Pretrial Order

Three to five months before trial, the clerk of the Tax Court will issue a notice setting the trial session calendar call date and the court will issue a pretrial order. Failure to follow the pretrial order may result in sanctions.[23] The common provisions of pretrial orders are addressed below:

- Stipulation of Facts. The pretrial order informs the parties that the Tax Court expects the parties to stipulate to undisputed facts. As discussed below, the court expects the parties to cooperate and to submit a Stipulation of Facts that includes all documents.
- Exchange of Documents. The pretrial order requires the parties to exchange all documents that they intend to introduce into evidence at trial 14 days prior to the calendar call, and submit all proposed trial exhibits to the Court. Some representatives and many self-represented intervenors ignore this requirement. When counsel objects to admission of the documents relying on the pretrial order's requirement to exchange documents prior to trial, the Tax Court, more often than not, will exclude the documents. So, a word to the wise: produce the documents you need in evidence to IRS counsel in a timely manner so that you do not violate the pretrial order, and be prepared to object to new evidence offered at trial by the intervenor.[24]
- Settlement of Issues. The pretrial order encourages the parties to meet and settle those issues upon which they can agree. The Tax Court is very interested in limiting the issues for trial to truly disputed issues.
- Pretrial Memorandum. The pretrial order directs each party to file a Pretrial Memorandum 21 days before trial, unless the case has been settled or a motion to dismiss for lack of prosecution is filed in its place. The Pretrial Memorandum generally includes the following:

---

[22] *See* I.R.C. § 7430(c)(4)(E)(ii)(I); *see also* Knudsen v. Comm'r, T.C. Memo. 2013-87.

[23] Tax Ct. R. 131(b); Rodriguez v. Comm'r, T.C. Memo. 2017-173.

[24] *See* Leith v. Comm'r, T.C. Memo. 2020-149 n. 11-12 (exhibits not exchanged were excluded at trial, and the court declined to re-open the record where intervenor failed to offer a compelling excuse for the failure).

- Issues. The Tax Court needs to know the issues for trial, as well as any issues that were raised in the petition or answer and have been resolved.
- Trial Time. The court expects the parties to estimate trial time. While this may seem like a trivial item, it is important to the court. Most trials in Tax Court take one to two hours. Some, of course, can take a day or longer. But, it is a mistake in the average case to put down a full day of trial based on a belief that the case would take that long in state court.
- Witnesses. The pretrial order requires the parties to identify the witnesses they intend to call and the general nature of their testimony. It is best to keep the description of the testimony brief.
- Factual Background. This requires judgment. The Pretrial memorandum does not constitute evidence and no purpose is served by detailing all the facts. Describe the essential facts so that you are telling the client's story, but remember that you will have a full opportunity to introduce facts and documents at trial.
- Legal Analysis. It is important to include a brief discussion of the controlling law and important cases, but it is not necessary to fully brief the legal arguments.
- Evidentiary Issues. If you anticipate evidentiary issues that you believe should be ruled on prior to trial, you can include the issues in the trial memorandum.

VI. The Stipulation of Facts

Nothing in Tax Court litigation is more important than the stipulation of facts. Tax Court Rule 91 requires the parties to stipulate, to the fullest extent, "all matters not privileged which are relevant to the pending case, regardless of whether such matters involve fact or opinion or the application of law to fact."[25] Matters which must be stipulated include all facts, documents and papers or contents or aspects thereof, and all evidence which fairly should not be in dispute.

The court expects the parties to prepare a document, suitably called the "Stipulation of Facts." This document includes individual paragraphs for each agreed fact or document; stipulated documents are attached as

[25] Tax Ct. R. 91.

numbered exhibits.[26] The stipulation must be filed 14 days before the calendar call, although a supplemental stipulation may be filed later. At the beginning of trial, the parties offer the Stipulation of Facts into evidence.

The Tax Court's stipulation process saves valuable court time. By stipulating a document, the offering party does not need to lay a foundation and introduce the document during the trial. When you stipulate an opponent's document, you are not agreeing that the contents are true, only that the document is authentic. For example, the income tax return in controversy is stipulated in almost every case, but the IRS is not agreeing that all the contents of the returns are true and correct. The IRS is only stipulating that the income tax return is a true copy of the return filed by the taxpayer. If the issue involves the amount of charitable contributions claimed on the taxpayer's return, the taxpayer cannot prove his or her case by introducing the tax return as proof. The taxpayer must offer documentary proof of the amounts spent for contributions. This documentary evidence should be included in the stipulation of facts.

At the time the stipulation of facts is prepared, a party can reserve an objection to a particular document. For example, if the taxpayer offers a letter from his or her doctor indicating that the taxpayer cannot work, the IRS can reserve a hearsay objection in the stipulation. This would be appropriate if the IRS attorney wanted to cross examine the doctor. Because the letter contains out of court statements, the IRS is entitled to cross examine the doctor. But, if the IRS attorney does not intend to cross examine the doctor, reserving a hearsay objection would not be productive.

While almost all documents must be stipulated, there are exceptions. A party is not required to stipulate a document that he or she does not believe is an authentic copy of the document. For example, a requesting spouse might refuse to stipulate to documents they reasonably believe were altered or forged by the intervenor.

While almost all documents must be stipulated, facts are treated differently in the stipulation process. To the extent that the parties can agree to facts it is in everyone's best interests to stipulate the facts. This can save valuable time. It should be possible to stipulate biographical information including important dates, such as the dates of house purchases and sales, divorces, and the birthdates of children. But either party can refuse to stipulate to any facts with which they fairly do not agree. For example, if the IRS does not believe the taxpayer's child lived with the taxpayer, the

---

[26] The numbering of trial exhibits is currently governed by the Tax Court's guidance document, *Documentary Evidence for Remote Proceedings*, posted on the Tax Court website at https://www.ustaxcourt.gov/resources/covid/documentary_evidence.pdf [https://perma.cc/XWH7-VE64]. *See also* Tax Ct. R. 91(b).

IRS does not have to stipulate to that fact. If the IRS proposes to stipulate that there was no abuse, but the taxpayer disagrees, then the taxpayer can refuse to stipulate there was no abuse. At trial, the parties are free to offer argument on these matters, and any evidence permitted under the record rule.

VII. Settlement

Innocent spouse cases are highly fact-specific, and it can be difficult to predict the outcome of a trial. Thus, hazards of litigation are often a basis for settlement. As always, any IRS offers of partial relief should be presented to your client for their consideration. After the case has been assigned to a trial judge, researching spousal relief opinions authored by your judge will assist you in settlement discussions as well as trial preparation. The U.S. Tax Court's online opinion search function is a valuable and free tool.[27]

VIII. Dealing with Intervenors

The nonrequesting spouse has the right to intervene as a party in the Tax Court case.[28] Tax Court Rule 325 charges the IRS with the task of notifying the nonrequesting spouse of this right within 60 days of service of the petition. Counsel for the petitioner should check the docket after this time has elapsed and remind counsel for respondent if the notice has not been sent. You do not want to discover on the eve of settlement (or trial) that the nonrequesting spouse never received notice of the petition.

As a party, the intervenor has all the same rights and obligations as the petitioner or respondent. If an intervenor opposes relief, the practitioner representing the requesting spouse must plan ahead to make full use of discovery mechanisms and position the case for trial. To the frustration of many requesting spouses, the intervenor can force a trial even if the IRS changes its position to support relief.[29]

---

[27] *See* https://dawson.ustaxcourt.gov/ (last visited Jan. 30, 2022).

[28] I.R.C. § 6015(e)(4).

[29] Corson v. Comm'r, 114 T.C. 354 (2000); King v. Comm'r, 11-5 T.C. 118 (2000).

Chapter 12: The Tax Court—Trial

I. Burden of Proof

A. In General

In Tax Court cases the burden of proof is generally on the taxpayer to prove the IRS determination is in error.[1] This is the case whether spousal relief is raised in a standalone case, as a defense to a deficiency, or as a collection alternative in CDP. A taxpayer meets their burden by offering proof that persuades the court by a preponderance of the evidence.[2] If at the time of trial the IRS supports the petitioner's claim for relief and the intervenor is the only opposing party, the burden of proof may shift to the intervenor.[3] It is likely, though, that the court will simply decide the case based on the preponderance of the evidence submitted by all parties.[4]

---

[1] Tax Ct. R. 142(a); Welch v. Helvering, 290 U.S. 111 (1933). Section 7491(a) allows the court to shift the burden to the IRS if the taxpayer meets certain conditions. This shift rarely occurs in the reported cases and counsel would be well advised to assume going into litigation that the taxpayer will bear the burden of proof. *See* Dunne v. Comm'r, T.C. Memo. 2008-63; Knudsen v. Comm'r, 131 T.C. 185 (2008), supplementing T.C. Memo. 2007-340.

[2] Stergios v. Comm'r, T.C. Memo. 2009-15; Porter v. Comm'r, 132 T.C. 203, 210 (2009).

[3] *See* Stergios v. Comm'r, T.C. Memo. 2009-15 (citing King v. Comm'r, 115 T.C. 118 (2000) and Corson v. Comm'r, 114 T.C. 354 (2000)).

[4] *See, e.g.*, Leith v. Comm'r, T.C. Memo. 2020-149.

The standard of review dictates what the taxpayer must prove. In deficiency and standalone cases, the court's standard of review is de novo,[5] so the requesting spouse must prove entitlement to spousal relief. In Collection Due Process cases where the underlying liability is not at issue, the standard of review is more deferential to the IRS: the court determines whether the Independent Office of Appeals abused its discretion.[6] Therefore, the taxpayer in a CDP case usually must prove that it was an abuse of discretion for the appeals officer to sustain the levy or the notice of lien.[7] However, if the underlying liability is properly at issue in the CDP proceeding because the taxpayer did not have a previous opportunity to dispute the liability, the standard of review is de novo.[8]

In some cases, it is possible that the Tax Court could assert jurisdiction under either I.R.C. § 6015(e) (standalone jurisdiction) or I.R.C. § 6330(d)(1) (CDP jurisdiction).[9] From the viewpoint of a requesting spouse, I.R.C. § 6015(e) provides a friendlier standard of review.

B. Section 6015(c) Cases

A requesting spouse must prove their eligibility for relief under I.R.C. § 6015(c), including their marital status and the amount of the deficiency allocable to each spouse.[10] The main exception to this rule is the knowledge element. If the IRS contests knowledge, the IRS must prove that the requesting spouse had actual knowledge, at the time they signed the return, of the item giving rise to the deficiency.[11] The IRS also has the burden of proof in two situations that occur less often: when it alleges that assets were transferred between the spouses as part of a fraudulent scheme, and when it alleges that allocation should be altered due to fraud.[12]

Intervention by the nonrequesting spouse complicates the burden of proof. If the nonrequesting spouse has intervened in the case and opposes relief, the Court will determine whether actual knowledge was proven "by a preponderance of the evidence as presented by all parties."[13]

---

[5] *See* Ax v. Comm'r, 146 T.C. 153 (2016) (regarding deficiency cases); I.R.C. § 6015(e)(7) (establishing the standard and scope of review for determinations made under § 6015).

[6] Sego v. Comm'r, 114 T.C. 604, 610 (2000).

[7] It is unclear whether the new standard and scope of review in I.R.C. § 6015(e)(7) impacts the court's review in CDP cases where spousal relief is raised as a collection alternative. The issue has not yet been litigated.

[8] Goza v. Comm'r, 114 T.C. 176, 181-82 (2000).

[9] Francel v. Comm'r, T.C. Memo. 2019-35.

[10] I.R.C. § 6015(c)(2); Treas. Reg. § 1.6015-3(d)(3).

[11] *See* I.R.C. § 6015(c)(3)(C).

[12] *See* I.R.C. § 6015(c)(3)(A)(ii), (d)(3)(C).

[13] Kitazono v. Comm'r, No. 3961-20 (Dec. 17, 2021); *see also* Young v. Comm'r, T.C. Memo. 2012-255, at *10.

II. The Opening Statement

The opening statement in Tax Court is important, but it is not nearly as important as the Stipulation of Facts, the Pretrial Memo, or preparing the requesting spouse to testify. Basically, the court wants to know the issues for trial and what the representative believes the proof will show. Recall that there is no jury and nothing said in the opening statement constitutes evidence; so it is neither necessary nor productive to go into minute detail about the proof. In some cases, the Court begins a trial by announcing that it has read the trial memoranda and counsel should limit or may waive opening statements.

A word about the issues in controversy may be of value. It is not particularly helpful to the Tax Court to state that the issue for trial is whether the requesting spouse is entitled to innocent spouse relief under I.R.C. § 6015(f). On the other hand, it is very helpful if you inform the Tax Court of the specific matters in dispute. For example:

- the requesting spouse seeks a review of the denial of equitable relief;
- the parties have stipulated and agree that the marital status and compliance-with-the-law factors favor relief; and
- the parties disagree on the economic hardship, significant benefit, and the legal responsibility factors.

This type of statement helps the court better understand what issues are in controversy.

III. The Most Important Witness

The most important witness in an innocent spouse case is the requesting spouse. However, the government may seek to limit your client's testimony under the administrative record rule.[14] It is important to address this before trial to the extent possible, to reduce uncertainty and stress on your client at trial.

A favorable ruling in Tax Court largely depends on the requesting spouse's credibility.[15] In *Wiest v. Commissioner*,[16] the Tax Court stressed the requesting spouse's credibility in reaching a decision favoring equitable relief, even

---

[14] *See supra* Chapter 11, III (Addressing the Record Rule).

[15] Credibility is pivotal. *See, e.g.*, Leith v. Comm'r, T.C. Memo. 2020-149; Richard v. Comm'r, T.C. Memo. 2011-144. In the underpayment case of *Alioto v. Comm'r*, T.C. Memo. 2008-185, the requesting spouse maintained that she believed that her husband, a successful lawyer, was financially solid and would pay any taxes due. The IRS presented testimony from a revenue officer that the requesting spouse would have known about liens on the couple's community property. In deciding the case for the requesting spouse, the court held that the requesting spouse's testimony more credible than the testimony of the revenue officer.

[16] T.C. Memo. 2003-91.

though it found no economic hardship. In *Merendino v. Commissioner*,[17] the Tax Court held against the requesting spouse and noted that, "[t]he record's direct contradiction of petitioner's statements strongly diminishes her credibility."

Thorough preparation strengthens your client's case. Tax Court judges are attentive listeners. If your client is hesitant, forgetful, or evasive, such characteristics can jeopardize a favorable ruling. Ensuring that your client's testimony is persuasive can be enhanced by thoughtful questions and thorough preparation. Prior to the trial date, you should sit down with your client and go over their testimony. This accomplishes two things: 1) the client will know and understand the questions that you intend to ask; and 2) you will know the answers. Hearing a surprise answer for the first time at trial has ruined many cases.

To the extent permitted by the court under the record rule, here are some areas to thoroughly develop:

- Biographical information, including age, date of marriage, date of divorce, and education. Family information, including names, ages, and any special needs of the client's children or other family members.
- Work history, including information about your client's current job and monthly income.
- Tax training or preparation—Did the requesting spouse have any tax training? What role did the requesting spouse play in the preparation of tax returns?
- Knowledge—What did the requesting spouse know on the date the return was filed? Was the nonrequesting spouse deceitful or secretive?
- Economic hardship—In addition to including supporting documents that establish the requesting spouse's basic living expenses for a month in the Stipulation of Facts, the requesting spouse should testify as to those expenses and any hardships that would be experienced by the collection of tax.
- Abuse—Develop facts regarding any physical or nonphysical abuse, especially abusive conduct regarding how financial decisions were made in the household and whether the requesting spouse was able to ask questions about the finances and the income tax returns.
- Financial Control—Develop facts regarding whether the nonrequesting spouse concealed financial information.

---

[17] T.C. Memo. 2006-2.

- Physical or mental health issues—Develop facts relating to physical and mental health conditions. Documents from medical providers and the Social Security Administration can be helpful.
- Significant benefit—Develop facts, if they exist, that establish that the tax savings or the refund were spent on normal support.

The nonrequesting spouse is also entitled to testify, and if they do, it is predictable that they will try to undermine the credibility of the requesting spouse.[18] It is important to ask the requesting spouse what they anticipate the nonrequesting spouse's testimony will be on key points. For example, if the requesting spouse alleges that the nonrequesting spouse did not allow her to see the bank statements or was unwilling to discuss his income, how does the requesting spouse think the nonrequesting spouse will respond to these allegations? Sometimes the requesting spouse has a good sense of the tack that the nonrequesting spouse will take and you will be better prepared on cross examination.[19]

Good trial work involves preparation, preparation, and preparation. Nothing is more important than preparing the requesting spouse to testify. It will also give you confidence about your case.

---

[18] Sometimes the nonrequesting spouse does not intervene, but the IRS calls them as a witness. This presents an important opportunity. If the nonrequesting spouse did not intervene then they are not a party. In this circumstance at the beginning of the trial, counsel for the requesting spouse should invoke the exclusionary rule. Tax Ct. R. 145. The rule is mandatory if invoked and Tax Court judges regularly grant these motions. This will force the nonrequesting spouse to sit outside the trial and prevent them from knowing the content of the requesting spouse's testimony.

[19] In *Sotuyo v. Comm'r*, T.C. Summ. Op. 2012-27, both the requesting spouse and the nonrequesting spouse sought innocent spouse relief. Both claimed that the other had been an abusive spouse. The court held that neither party had shown they were entitled to the abuse factor. It is possible that with better preparation the abuse factor could have been proven.

Chapter 13: Obtaining a Refund from the IRS

I. The Refund

A key part of analyzing a client's claim for innocent spouse relief is their eligibility to receive a refund for payments they already made to the IRS towards the joint liability. The refund issue is generally not ready for resolution until the IRS or a court grants relief under § 6015, but at that time, the IRS will be bound to return payments that meet the general rules for refund claims. Accordingly, it is important to file a Form 8857 following the same time rules that apply for any administrative refund claim and to ensure that the application contains sufficient information to put the IRS on notice that the client is seeking a refund in addition to relief from any remaining joint liability.[1]

When taxpayers do not pay their liabilities to the IRS, the agency will offset any refunds due for ongoing tax years until the liability is paid. This means that several payments, through refund offset, may have been made over several years. Thus, your client's interests not only include relief from any joint liabilities that remain unpaid, but include recovering any refunds that have been applied to the joint tax years in controversy.

---

[1] Treas. Reg. § 301.6402-2(b)(1) (as amended in 2013).

II. Statutory Framework

In addition to the general rules applicable to tax refunds, refunds in innocent spouse cases are limited to overpayments resulting from a grant of relief under § 6015.[2] Thus, if additional refunds are sought due to issues not involving innocent spouse relief, the taxpayer must timely file independent administrative claims for refund based on those issues.

III. General Rules for All Refunds

A timely claim for refund must inform the IRS that a refund is being asserted, include the grounds for the refund, and provide sufficient facts so that the IRS can examine the merits of the claim.[3] Generally, a claim for refund must be filed within three years from the date the return is filed or within two years from the time the tax is paid.[4]

In addition, the claim must meet the requirements of § 6511(a) and (b) which impose limitations on the time for filing claims and the amounts of the claims. The amount of any refund is limited to payments made during the three-year period following the due date of the return (the three-year look back period) and to the two-year period from the date of payment of any tax (the two-year look back period).

IV. Limitations Applicable to Innocent Spouse Cases

Section 6015 authorizes credits and refunds in innocent spouse cases only in those cases in which a taxpayer is granted innocent spouse relief.[5] Further, § 6015(g)(1) makes applicable the rules contained in §§ 6511, 6512(b), 7121 and 7122 to all refunds in § 6015 cases.[6] Finally, Congress expressly provided that no refunds are allowable under § 6015(c), which addresses separate liability elections. Refunds are only available where the taxpayer is granted relief under subsections (b) or (f). If the IRS is resisting a claim for refund, it is wise to closely examine the applicable statutes and the cases to see if the IRS position is sound. At the first client meeting or shortly thereafter, it is necessary to identify the time that payments were made. Any delay in filing a refund claim on some or all the prior payments

---

[2] I.R.C. § 6015(g)(1).

[3] *See* Chicago Milwaukee Corp. v. United States, 40 F.3d 373, 375 (Fed Cir. 1994); Treas. Reg. § 301.6402-2(b)(1).

[4] I.R.C. § 6511(a).

[5] I.R.C. § 6015(g)(1).

[6] I.R.C. § 6511 contains rules limiting the time to file refunds and rules limiting the amount of refunds. § 6512(b) involves refunds in deficiency proceedings. § 7121 applies to closing agreements and § 7122 involves compromises. Most cases involve the limitations under § 6511.

made could result in the claim being denied for timeliness, even if § 6015 relief is otherwise granted.[7]

Normally, filing a Form 8857 which includes a claim for refund for a particular year is sufficient. This will generally satisfy the requirement that the IRS be notified that a refund claim is being made, the grounds for the claim, and the facts surrounding the claim. The failure to timely raise and argue the claim can result in the denial of the claim.[8]

---

[7] *See* I.R.C. § 6511.

[8] *See Ewing III*, 439 F.3d 1009 (9th Cir. 2006).

Chapter 14: Collection Alternatives When Innocent Spouse Fails

I. Collections Overview

The IRS approaches collections from the understandable premise that people should pay their taxes on time. The collection process is largely automated. When taxes are not paid, computer systems send out a stream of collection notices and then search for income and assets to levy.[1] It is the individual's responsibility to speak up and tell the IRS if they qualify for an alternative to full payment.

A taxpayer's most important opportunity to speak up is when they receive a Collection Due Process ("CDP") notice. Two CDP notices may be received for each tax liability: one is required before the IRS can levy on income or assets, and one is required after the IRS files a notice of federal tax lien.[2] A CDP notice gives the taxpayer 30 days to request a hearing

---

[1] The IRS Taxpayer Advocate Service has a helpful roadmap of the collection process online at https://www.taxpayeradvocate.irs.gov/get-help/roadmap/. For an in-depth treatment of tax collection procedure and collection alternatives, see chapters 10 through 12 of Effectively Representing Your Client Before the IRS (ABA 8th Ed. 2021).

[2] I.R.C. §§ 6330(a)(2) (levy); 6320(a)(2) (lien).

with the IRS Independent Office of Appeals.[3] CDP is important because it allows taxpayers to appeal their case to the Tax Court if they do not reach an agreement with Appeals. However, do not despair if your client's appeal deadline has passed.[4] The IRS will always consider a proposed collection alternative from a taxpayer.

When assisting your client with IRS collections you will most likely be interacting with employees at an IRS campus by phone, fax, and mail. Relatively few taxpayers these days receive the personal attention of a revenue officer. To request a collection alternative or obtain information about your client's account, you can call the IRS Practitioner Priority Service ("PPS").[5] You may be transferred multiple times before you reach someone who can assist you; be prepared to wait on hold.

The IRS uses Form 433, Collection Information Statement ("CIS"), to evaluate taxpayer requests for collection alternatives based on ability to pay.[6] Consistent with its philosophy on collections, the IRS starts its evaluation by determining whether the taxpayer can full pay or make a lump sum payment from assets. If not, the IRS calculates the taxpayer's ability to make monthly payments by taking their gross income and subtracting allowable expenses. Closely review the Collection Financial Standards and the Financial Analysis Handbook to understand how the IRS views different types of expenses.[7] These internal sources allow the representative to anticipate likely questions or objections to the solution proposed by the taxpayer.

A taxpayer must be current on their filing and payment obligations for the years following the year(s) at issue in order to be eligible for most collection alternatives. The one exception is when economic hardship is shown, because the IRS is prohibited from enforced collection in hardship situations.[8]

---

[3] I.R.C. §§ 6330(a)(3)(B) (levy); 6320(a)(3)(B) (lien). Be aware that the IRS sends other notices titled "Notice of Intent to Levy" which are not CDP notices; they do not give the right to a hearing with IRS Appeals. *See* Keith Fogg, *Causing Less Work for Themselves and Others*, PROCEDURALLY TAXING (Feb. 10, 2022), *available at* https://perma.cc/DB52-BS6Z.

[4] An "equivalent" hearing can be requested within one year of the CDP notice. Treas. Reg. § 301.6320-1(i), Q&A-I17. This provides the opportunity to discuss the case with IRS Appeals, but there is no appeal to the Tax Court.

[5] The current PPS phone number is 866-860-4259. For helpful information about contacting the IRS, see Practitioner Priority Service, https://www.irs.gov/tax-professionals/practitioner-priority-service-r (last visited Mar. 3, 2022).

[6] Form 433 comes in several variations: Form 433-F is the short form, used in most low-income taxpayer cases. Form 433-A is the "regular" form. There are also Forms 433 for offers in compromise and for business entities. All are available at irs.gov/forms.

[7] *See* I.R.M. 5.15.1 (11-22-21). The I.R.M. links to the collection financial standards. Or, go to IRS.gov and type "collection financial standards" into the search bar.

[8] See I.R.C. § 6343(a)(1)(D); Vinatieri v. Comm'r, 133 T.C. 392 (2009).

When jointly liable spouses separate, the IRS's collection machinery will engage against both individuals. The IRS will only collect the tax liability once, however. This means that the person who is easiest to collect from usually ends up paying the debt. With prompt action you may be able to protect your client's assets and income.

II. Collection Complications for Separated Spouses

A. Account Mirroring

After a tax return is filed, the IRS tracks the liability and any activity on the account (such as payments, the filing of lien notices, and CDP appeals) in its computer systems.[9] For individuals, this information is reflected on the Form 1040 account transcript available to taxpayers and authorized representatives. A joint tax return will generate an identical account transcript for each spouse.

When spouses with a joint return go their separate ways, under certain situations the IRS will split the joint account into two "separate assessment" accounts, so that it can accurately track the liabilities and post-assessment activities (and associated legal deadlines) applicable to each spouse. This is called mirroring or spitting the account.[10] The I.R.M. explains that this can be done when one of the following applies:

- Collection action is prohibited against only one spouse.
- Each spouse is liable for different amounts.
- Each spouse has different penalty and/or interest suspension periods.
- Each spouse has a different statute of limitations.[11]

Among other situations, the IRS should mirror joint accounts:

- After innocent spouse relief has been granted;[12]
- When only one spouse files a bankruptcy petition;[13] and

[9] Tax accounts are often referred to in the I.R.M. by their Master File Tax Account Code ("MFT"). Most individual income tax (Form 1040) accounts are coded as MFT 30. *See* Tax Modules, I.R.M. 21.2.1.2.3 (10-01-2011).

[10] *See generally* Split Spousal Assessments, I.R.M. 21.6.8. When a joint account is mirrored, the spouses' separate liabilities are generally moved from a joint MFT 30 module to separate MFT 31 modules. Background, I.R.M. 25.15.15.1.1 (10-16-2020).

[11] Split Spousal Assessments Overview, I.R.M. 21.6.8.2 (10-01-2016).

[12] Background, I.R.M. 25.15.15.1.1 (10-16-2020); *but see* Accounts That Cannot Be Mirrored, I.R.M. Exhibit 25.15.18-2.

[13] What is MFT 31 / MFT 65, I.R.M. 21.6.8.4 (10-01-2015) (listing triggering events).

- When one spouse obtains a collection alternative separately from the other spouse (including an offer in compromise, installment agreement, or currently not collectible).[14]

Despite this policy, it is common in our experience for accounts that should be mirrored to remain joint for quite some time. In some cases the IRS is not aware that the situation warrants mirroring, for example when one spouse establishes a "joint" installment agreement without the other's knowledge. Carefully consider the pros and cons of bringing this to the IRS's attention.

After accounts are mirrored, the 1040 account transcript will be zeroed out, showing no liability. This zero balance has perplexed many novice representatives. Your Form 2848 must list "1040 Separate Assessment—Separation of Liability" as an authorized matter below "1040—Income," to ensure that you have access to both the "regular" 1040 account transcript and the separate assessment transcript.

B. Obtaining Information About Payments by the Other Spouse

After accounts have been mirrored, you can no longer get information about collection activities with respect to the other spouse by obtaining the account transcript. The separate assessment transcript of the other spouse is not available to you. Conversely your client's separate account transcript is not available to their (ex-)spouse. Also, the IRS does not disclose personal information to separated spouses, including a taxpayer's new name, address, or income.[15]

Despite these limits, each spouse on a joint tax return still has the right to information about the collection activities of the IRS with respect to the other spouse, including the amount collected.[16] IRS employees do not always understand their duty to disclose collection information on mirrored accounts,[17] so persistence may be needed to obtain the information to which your client is entitled.

---

[14] *Id.*

[15] *See* Disclosing Taxpayer Data, I.R.M. 21.6.8.3 (10-01-2021); *see also* Disclosure of Collection Activities with Respect to Joint Returns, I.R.M. 11.3.2.4.1.1 (09-17-2020); I.R.C. § 6103(e)(7) Disclosure Procedures, I.R.M. 5.1.22.4.1 (08-01-2019).

[16] I.R.C. § 6103(e)(1)(B), (e)(7), (e)(8). Spouses generally have the right to return information concerning joint returns under I.R.C. § 6103(e)(7), because they are authorized under § 6103(e)(1)(B). In addition, I.R.C. § 6103(e)(8) entitles spouses to collection information concerning deficiencies. The IRS appears to view this provision as overlapping with the information already available as a general matter. Disclosure of Collection Activities with Respect to Joint Returns, I.R.M. 11.3.2.4.1.1(2) (09-17-2020).

[17] *See* Treasury Inspector General for Tax Administration, *Fiscal Year 2021 Statutory Review of Disclosure of Collection Activity With Respect to Joint Returns*, Report No. 2021-30-050 (Aug. 16, 2021).

Taxpayers who are survivors of domestic violence may request that a "victim of domestic violence" indicator be placed on their IRS account.[18] This indicator does not change the applicable disclosure laws, of course, but IRS employees may treat your client with more sensitivity and may take more care when authenticating callers attempting to access information about the account.

C. The Collection Statute Expiration Date

The IRS generally has ten years after assessment to collect a tax liability.[19] The collection period can be extended by many acts, including filing bankruptcy, submitting an offer in compromise, requesting an installment agreement, filing a collection due process appeal, and requesting innocent spouse relief.[20] The suspension period for each tolling event varies. For example, the collection statute expiration date ("CSED") is extended while a taxpayer's request for an installment agreement is pending.[21] If the request is accepted by the IRS, the CSED resumes running and continues running while the agreement is in effect.

Review your client's joint and separate assessment account transcripts for items that toll the CSED and perform your own calculations. The CSED in the IRS computer system is sometimes incorrect. There is particular danger of an incorrect CSED when an installment agreement has been requested.[22]

III. Collection Alternatives

A. Hardship: Currently Not Collectible Status and Offset Bypass Refunds

If your client cannot afford to make payments to the IRS while also paying their basic necessary living expenses, they should qualify for Currently Not Collectible ("CNC") hardship status. The criteria are set out in the I.R.M.[23]

---

[18] *See* Victim of Domestic Violence (VODV), I.R.M. 25.15.18.9.2.6 (03-20-2019). *See also* IRS Form 8857, Question 23a (Rev. 6-2021) (noting that a code will be placed on the requesting spouse's separate account if they indicate they are a victim of abuse, unless otherwise requested).

[19] I.R.C. § 6502.

[20] I.R.C. §§ 6503(h); 6331(k)(1); 6331(k)(2); 6330(e); 6015(e)(1)(B), (e)(2). These are common acts that suspend the CSED; there are others in the Code. *See, e.g.*, I.R.C. § 6503(b)-(c); *see also* Conditions Postponing Collection or Suspending the 10 Year Collection Period, I.R.M. 25.6.1.12.2.1 (07-09-2021); Rachel Radspinner and Derek B. Wagner, *Spotting Statutes of Limitations Issues in Assessment and Collection Matters*, in Effectively Representing Your Client Before the IRS (ABA 8th Ed. 2021).

[21] I.R.C. § 6331(k)(2), (k)(3), (i)(5).

[22] *See* Keith Fogg, *More Clarity on CSED Problem*, Procedurally Taxing (Jul. 9, 2021), https://perma.cc/K2ZZ-RKAH (citing to Taxpayer Advocate Service reports).

[23] *See* Currently Not Collectible, I.R.M. 5.16.1.

The IRS has discretion to request documents supporting your client's CNC application. For low-income taxpayers, common documents requested are

- Form 433-F;
- last paystub;
- last bank statement;
- last car loan statement;
- life insurance statement (showing cash value); and
- documents supporting any expenses claimed above the IRS standards.

To obtain CNC for your client, call the IRS and ask for it. This is the fastest way to obtain relief for your client. Be prepared to give your client's CIS to the IRS verbally, and to fax substantiating documents to the customer service representative. If you do not have all the requested documents, the representative will direct you to mail the CIS and supporting documents to the IRS. This takes longer, but the IRS should be able to enter a collection hold allowing time for the documents to be considered.

In some extreme hardship situations, a CIS is not required.[24] If your client is incarcerated, has only unemployment or public benefits income, or has no income at all, they may be eligible for CNC without providing a full CIS. Call the IRS and explain the situation.

It can be helpful to obtain CNC hardship status for a new client as an interim measure. This will protect your client against most collection action while you investigate and prepare to request a permanent solution such as spousal relief or an offer in compromise. However, be aware that a CNC request can trigger the IRS to file a notice of federal tax lien (NFTL). The current threshold for a NFTL is $10,000 in total IRS liabilities.[25]

CNC is temporary, so third-party information reporting or tax return information can trigger a re-evaluation of CNC status. However, CNC can effectively be permanent if your client is disabled or retired, and their financial situation will not improve.

Note that CNC status does not stop the IRS from offsetting tax refunds under I.R.C. § 6402. To receive a federal tax refund while owing an IRS debt, the taxpayer must contact the IRS and request an offset bypass refund ("OBR") on hardship grounds.[26] OBRs can be requested by calling the

---

[24] *See* I.R.M. 5.16.1.2.9(6) (09-18-2018).

[25] *See* Notice of Lien Determinations, I.R.M. 5.12.2 (11-9-2015).

[26] The IRS has no discretion to bypass an offset for non-IRS debt such as child support. *See* Keith Fogg, *Requesting an Offset Bypass Refund and Tracing Offsets to Non-IRS Sources*, PROCEDURALLY TAXING (Dec. 9, 2015), https://perma.cc/UYK3-LJ87.

IRS directly[27] or by requesting assistance from the IRS Taxpayer Advocate Service.[28]

The IRS's stated hardship threshold to receive an OBR is the inability to pay basic living expenses.[29] However, in practice many IRS employees require a higher level of hardship to be met and documented with certainty before they will release a refund.[30] For example, a utility shutoff notice, eviction or foreclosure notice, or other similar document combined with a CIS may be requested. Do not hesitate to advocate for your client based on the I.R.M., but be prepared for scrutiny.

If a taxpayer proves hardship in a certain amount (such as the amount needed to prevent eviction), the IRS will release the dollar amount proven and offset the rest of the tax refund.[31]

Timing is a tricky consideration with OBRs. An OBR must be requested before the tax return has been processed. Refunds that have already offset cannot usually be retrieved.[32] You must coordinate with your client and contact the IRS immediately after the return is filed for the OBR to succeed. OBRs are usually a mad scramble, but the payoff of saving your client's refund can be enormous.

B. Installment Agreements

There are several types of installment agreements ("IA"s).[33] The most important distinction is between IAs that require a CIS, and those that do not.

If your client's balance due and monthly payment will support a guaranteed[34] or streamlined[35] IA, there is no need to provide financial information to the IRS. A longstanding threshold for streamlined IAs has been that the monthly payment equals or exceeds the total liability divided by 72. However, the government regularly changes its standards for streamlined IAs, so it is best to consult the IRS website and I.R.M. frequently. These

---

[27] Offset Bypass Refund (OBR), I.R.M. 21.4.6.5.11.1(3) (11-08-2017).

[28] *See* IRS Publication 1546, *Taxpayer Advocate Service – Your Voice at the IRS*. The fastest way to request TAS assistance is to fax Form 911 with supporting documents, Form 2848, and a persuasive cover letter to your local TAS office.

[29] Offset Bypass Refund (OBR), I.R.M. 21.4.6.5.11.1(1) (11-08-2017).

[30] The Treasury Inspector General for Tax Administration has raised concerns about inconsistent standards for OBRs within the Taxpayer Advocate Service. *See* Leslie Book, *TIGTA Report Criticizes TAS's Approach to Offset Bypass Refunds*, Procedurally Taxing (Oct. 20, 2020), https://perma.cc/F8FB-NJ32.

[31] Offset Bypass Refund (OBR), I.R.M. 21.4.6.5.11.1(14) (11-08-2017).

[32] *See* Offset Bypass Refund (OBR), I.R.M. 21.4.6.5.11.1 (11-08-2017).

[33] *See* Installment Agreements, I.R.M. 5.14 (various). IAs are authorized by I.R.C. § 6159.

[34] *See* I.R.C. § 6159(c); Guaranteed Installment Agreements, I.R.M. 5.14.5.3 (10-14-2021).

[35] *See* Streamlined Installment Agreements, I.R.M. 5.14.5.2 (10-14-2021).

types of IAs are approved quickly, and they can be requested on IRS.gov, over the phone, or by mailing Form 9465 to the address on your client's last IRS bill.

If your client cannot afford a streamlined IA payment, you will need to provide a CIS and any supporting documents requested by the IRS.[36] Follow the procedure described above for requesting CNC, but note that the IRS usually requires more supporting documents to accept a "partial-pay" IA than to accept a CNC request. While you can request a partial pay IA by mail, it is helpful to call first to clarify what documents the IRS wants to see. The documents requested will depend on your client's CIS, which will be thoroughly scrutinized.

The IRS may file a notice of federal tax lien as a condition of the IA, and it will continue to offset tax refunds while an IA is in place, but your client will be protected from levy by I.R.C. § 6331(k).

C. *Offers in Compromise*

I.R.C. § 7122 allows the IRS to compromise federal tax debts. The most common basis for compromise is doubt as to collectability.[37] When making an offer in compromise ("OIC") based on doubt as to collectability, the goal is to demonstrate that your client lacks the assets and income to fully pay the liability and convince the IRS that it is in the best interests of the government to settle for a lesser amount. Generally, taxpayers must offer to pay at least their reasonable collection potential ("RCP").[38] RCP includes net realizable equity in assets plus available future income over the next 12 or 24 months, depending on how quickly the offer will be paid.[39]

RCP is hypothetical; it represents what the government could collect if it employed its extraordinary collection powers to the maximum extent possible. The fact that the IRS will not in practice seize most debtors' personal property or homes does not exclude those assets from the calculation. Because of this, it is usually very difficult for a taxpayer with equity (most often in a home or retirement account) to afford the minimum offer required by the IRS. But, an OIC can be an excellent solution for a taxpayer without much equity in assets. The income piece of the RCP equation can also be a hurdle if the taxpayer has expenses that the IRS does not consider "allowable."

---

36 *See generally* I.R.M. 5.14.2 (4-26-2019).

37 Grounds for compromise are set out in Treas. Reg. § 301.7122-1(b).

38 Policy, I.R.M. 5.8.1.2.2(4) (04-20-2021) (citing Policy Statement 5-100, I.R.M. 1.2.1.6.17 (01-30-1992)).

39 Components of Collectibility, I.R.M. 5.8.4.3.1 (04-30-2015); *see also* Doubt as to Collectibility, I.R.M. 5.8.4.3(2) (09-24-2020) (explaining RCP).

In some situations the IRS can be persuaded to disregard equity in assets on hardship or public policy grounds, but this requires persuasive advocacy and will not be possible in all cases.[40] The regulations and the I.R.M. contain helpful examples.[41] The most common is when equity in assets will be needed to provide for basic living expenses of the taxpayer and their dependents.

IRS Form 656-B, Offer in Compromise Booklet, contains all the necessary forms and helpfully walks through the minimum offer calculation.[42] The booklet also has instructions for submitting the OIC and a checklist of documents to attach. However, beware of relying solely on the IRS forms. Some of the statutory asset exclusions in I.R.C. § 6334 are listed on Form 433-A (OIC) but some are not.[43] It is also important to review the I.R.M. carefully to ensure that your financial analysis is in line with the minimum that will be acceptable to the IRS. For example, the form does not account for the shared expense calculations that must be provided when expenses are shared with a non-liable taxpayer (for example, a new spouse).[44] In places where the Form 433-A (OIC) does not accurately reflect your client's reasonable collection potential, you will need to make a note and attach an explanation. An attachment is usually needed to fully set out the taxpayer's allowable expenses and accurate collection potential.

Compromise is discretionary; the IRS can deny an offer as not in the best interest of the government even if the taxpayer offers their RCP.[45] For this reason, it is important to include information in your offer packet that personalizes your client, gives context for their tax troubles, and addresses any questions that are likely to arise in the mind of a skeptical IRS employee. A statement signed by your client under penalty of perjury is very helpful.

---

[40] When a taxpayer offers less than their RCP on hardship grounds, it is called either Doubt as to Collectibility with Special Circumstances, or Effective Tax Administration–Hardship. The difference lies in how RCP compares to the total liability. If RCP is equal to or greater than the liability, the offer is considered under Effective Tax Administration. If RCP is less than the total owed, the offer is considered under Doubt as to Collectibility. Legal Basis for Effective Tax Administration Offer, I.R.M. 5.8.11.3 (10-04-2019). The analysis is the same in both cases. Consideration of Doubt as to Collectibility Offers, I.R.M. 8.23.3.1(3) (08-18-2017) ("An offer based upon doubt as to collectibility with "special circumstances" will be evaluated using the same criteria as an ETA offer.").

[41] *See* Treas. Reg. § 301.7122-1(c)(3); Economic Hardship, I.R.M. 5.8.11.3.1 (10-04-2019); Public Policy or Equity Compelling Factors, I.R.M. 5.8.11.3.2.1 (10-04-2019).

[42] *See also* Rev. Proc. 2003-71, 2003-36 I.R.B. 517 (Sept. 8, 2003) (setting out OIC submission and processing procedures).

[43] For example, the exclusion for personal effects under I.R.C. § 6334(a)(2) is listed on page 4 of Form 433-A (OIC) (Rev. 4-2021), but the exclusion for tools of the trade under I.R.C. § 6334(a)(3) is not. The administrative asset exclusions created by the IRS for cash and vehicles are listed on the form.

[44] *See* Shared Expenses, I.R.M. 5.8.5.24 (09-24-2021).

[45] Not in the Best Interest of the Government Rejection, I.R.M. 5.8.7.7.1(1) (12-20-2018).

Your cover letter should present the offer and explain why it qualifies for acceptance under the IRM.

D. Bankruptcy

Bankruptcy may provide your client with full relief from their IRS debts. Conversely, if your client's (ex-)spouse filed a bankruptcy petition on their own, bankruptcy may relieve that person of the joint liability, leaving your client on the hook. When assisting a client with a joint debt, it is a good idea to search for bankruptcy filings by both spouses.[46]

To evaluate whether bankruptcy discharge is a possibility for your client, you will need their account transcripts (both 1040 and 1040 Separate Assessment transcripts, if available) for the past ten years, plus any older years with outstanding liabilities.

The threshold requirements for dischargeability of an individual's federal income tax debt in a Chapter 7 bankruptcy are:

- the tax return was due more than three years before the bankruptcy petition is filed;[47]
- the tax return was filed at least two years before the bankruptcy petition is filed;[48]
- the tax was assessed more than 240 days before the bankruptcy petition is filed;[49] and
- the liability does not stem from a substitute tax return by the IRS under I.R.C. § 6020(b).[50]

There are other bankruptcy law requirements that must be met for a successful discharge, and the determination of whether bankruptcy is a good option for your client can be complicated.[51] However, if your client's tax liabilities pass the four basic tests above, or if your client has significant nontax debts, you may want to refer your client to a bankruptcy attorney for a consultation.

---

[46] Bankruptcy records are available through the federal judiciary's Public Access to Court Electronic Records ("PACER") system, at https://pacer.uscourts.gov/.

[47] 11 U.S.C. § 507(a)(8)(A)(i).

[48] 11 U.S.C. § 523(a)(1)(B).

[49] 11 U.S.C. § 507(a)(8)(A)(ii). The 240-day period is tolled while a stay of collections is in effect. *Id.* It is important to carefully calculate this date taking into account innocent spouse requests and other actions that stay collections.

[50] 11 U.S.C. § 523(a)(*) (hanging paragraph following 11 U.S.C. § 523(a)(19)). The fifth, tenth, and first circuits go beyond this position and require that the tax return have been filed on time. *See* McCoy v. Miss. State Tax Comm'n (In re McCoy), 666 F.3d 924 (5th Cir. 2012); Mallo v. IRS (In re Mallo), 774 F.3d 1313 (10th Cir. 2014); Fahey v. IRS, 779 F.3d 1 (1st Cir. 2015).

[51] *See generally* Kenneth C. Weil and Bradley D. Jones, *Utilizing Bankruptcy to Reduce Outstanding Tax Debts*, in Effectively Representing Your Client Before the IRS (ABA 8th Ed. 2021).

Chapter 15: State Innocent Spouse Relief

I. Overview

Obtaining federal innocent spouse relief is usually a partial victory for the client. More often than not, a joint liability is also present on the client's state tax return, if they are in a state that has personal income tax. The problems that led to the federal assessment are also likely to appear on the state tax return. It is a regular practice of the IRS to inform state tax authorities when a deficiency has been assessed on the federal return. The state will then impose its own assessment on the state return.

If a taxpayer has obtained innocent spouse relief for a given year on the federal return, there is no automatic relief on the state side. That is because there is no mechanism for the IRS to inform the state tax authorities that innocent spouse relief has been granted. Even if such a mechanism were in place, it would be inconsistent because different states have different requirements for innocent spouse relief which may or may not track federal laws and guidelines. Some states do not offer any type of innocent spouse relief at all.

Determining if a client also has a joint liability on their state income taxes starts with a review of the state returns. States vary widely in accessibility to past account data. In Massachusetts, for example, there are no comprehensive "account transcripts" that a practitioner can access to review past tax years. However, the client can access a list of years for which they owe money, and the outstanding balance, by creating an online account through the Department of Revenue website. This is a starting point for the practitioner.

Conversely, if your client only lived during the tax years at issue in one of the nine states that has no state income tax (and did not file joint returns in any other state) then such analysis is unnecessary.

II. Questions to Ask to Evaluate the Need for State Action

- Does your client have a state tax liability for a year in which they believe they are an innocent spouse?
- Does the state in question have innocent spouse relief provisions?
- Do the state provisions track federal law?
- Does the state provision actually incorporate the federal law into its own analysis for relief?
- Does the state provision declare that it will act only after, and according to, a federal determination?
- Does your client meet the requirements of the state provisions?
- Do the state provisions allow for relief for underpayment, as well as understatement, of tax?
- What processes does the state require to submit an innocent spouse claim?
- Will the state offer a refund?

III. Survey of State Law on Relief from Joint and Several Liability as of 2021

The following list is a basic review of relief provisions in each state. Further research into a given state's provisions by the practitioner, including regulations, guidance documents, and forms is required to actually analyze whether a client may qualify in a given state.

1. *Alabama*

Alabama law states that if a taxpayer has received relief for a federal joint return under § 6015(b), (c), or (f), then that taxpayer will also receive relief from joint liability on their Alabama joint return. Ala. Code § 40-18-27(e).

In addition, Alabama has a state regulation providing for relief similar to the federal "b" relief provision. Presumably this would apply if someone was seeking innocent spouse relief only on their state return. Under that provision, called the "Innocent Spouse Rule," relief applies if there was an understatement of tax, the taxpayer shows they did not know or have reason to know of the understatement, and that it would be inequitable to hold them liable. *See* ALA. ADMIN. CODE 810-3-27-01.

2. *Alaska*

Alaska has no personal income tax.

3. *Arizona*

Arizona has statutory provisions that track the language of federal "b" and "c" relief. *See* ARIZ. CODE § 42-2201. Additionally, the 2017 Arizona revised statutes include an equitable relief provision, allowing for relief with a facts and circumstances analysis. ARIZ. REV. STATE. ANN. 42-2074.

NOTE: Arizona is a community property state and so, in the context of seeking federal relief, an applicant may apply for relief under I.R.C. § 66 (c).

4. *Arkansas*

Arkansas has a statute entitled "Relief of Spouse from Liability," which applies only to underpayments attributable to one spouse. ARK. CODE ANN. § 26-18-708.

The statute's requirements for relief are whether the requesting spouse significantly benefited from the understatement of tax, whether the requesting spouse knew or had reason to know about the understatement, and whether the facts and circumstances would make it be inequitable to hold the requesting spouse liable.

Of further note, Arkansas defines "reason to know" as "whether a reasonably prudent person would have known that an understatement was made." It defines an understatement "attributable to" one spouse as the result of actions taken or information supplied by that spouse."

5. *California*

California's relevant statute provides for all three versions of federal relief on the state level. It requires the taxpayer to include any federal determination of relief for the same tax years in question. CAL REV. & TAX CODE § 18533.

Economic hardship, which the federal Rev. Proc. 2013-34 treats as neutral if not present, is a negative factor under California regulations if not present. *See* CAL. CODE REGS. 18 § 4903.

Additionally, in divorce proceedings in California, the state court is authorized to "revise" the couple's joint and several liabilities for state taxes, so long as such an order does not "relieve a spouse of tax liability on income earned by or subject to the exclusive management of that spouse." CAL REV. & TAX CODE § 19006(b).

NOTE: California is a community property state and so, in the context of seeking federal relief, an applicant may apply for relief under I.R.C. § 66(c).

6. ***Colorado***

Colorado law states that it will offer "comparable" relief if a taxpayer has been granted federal relief under § 6015. It is silent as to whether a taxpayer can seek independent state relief. COLO. REV. STATE. ANN. § 39-22-107.5.

7. ***Connecticut***

Connecticut's relevant statute provides for all three versions of federal relief on the state level. CONN. GEN. STAT. § 12-702a(a).

8. ***Delaware***

Delaware does not have provisions for relief from joint income tax liability.

9. ***District of Columbia***

The District of Columbia provides for the separation of "delinquent taxes" between spouses. The statute mandates the automatic separation of "the amount due to the spouse who owes delinquent taxes from the spouse who does not owe delinquent taxes based upon the proportion of gross income of each spouse." Furthermore, the statute provides that "the tax refund of the spouse who does not owe delinquent taxes shall not be credited against the liability of the spouse who owes delinquent taxes." This provision includes domestic partners who, in D.C., are allowed to file joint income tax returns. D.C. CODE ANN. § 47-4432.

10. ***Florida***

Florida has no personal income tax.

11. ***Georgia***

Georgia law contains a statute that tracks the language and requirements of federal "b" relief. However, if someone receives relief on their corresponding federal return, they will be entitled to relief on their Georgia return even if it was granted under other federal relief provisions. GA. CODE ANN. § 48-6-86.

12. ***Hawaii***

Hawaii directly incorporates § 6015 into its state law. HAW. REV. STAT. ANN. § 235-2.45(1)(k).

13. *Idaho*

Idaho law states that it will provide relief on a joint return if the taxpayer obtained federal relief. It is silent as to whether a taxpayer can seek independent state relief. IDAHO CODE ANN. § 63-3050A.

NOTE: Idaho is a community property state and so, in the context of seeking federal relief, an applicant may apply for relief under I.R.C. § 66 (c).

14. *Illinois*

Illinois law provides that for joint income tax liabilities arising from returns prior to August 13, 1999, a taxpayer may seek relief from the liability by showing proof they had obtained relief from the IRS on their federal return pursuant to the former § 6013(e). If they only had a state, not a federal liability, prior to August 13, 1999, then the state may evaluate their claim for relief under the provisions of § 6013(e).

For liabilities arising after August 13, 1999, a taxpayer may seek relief by applying for federal relief under § 6015 and notifying the state's Department of Revenue of that election. If they have not applied for federal relief, then they may apply for relief directly to the state Department of Revenue according to a manner prescribed by the department. This cannot be done, however, if the couple had exchanged assets to avoid paying the liability. 35 ILL. COMP. STAT. ANN. 5/502.

15. *Indiana*

Indiana does not impose joint and several liability on joint income tax returns. Spouses filing a joint return in Indiana are protected from initially incurring income tax from items attributed to the other spouse. IND. CODE § 6-3-4-2. Despite this protection, the state does routinely try to collect tax liabilities from both spouses, without first determining which spouse is responsible for which portion of the liability. The state's Department of Revenue therefore has a form and procedure for applying for "Innocent Spouse Relief," but its purpose is to show the state how the liability should be allocated, which is a matter of right for the taxpayer.[1]

16. *Iowa*

Iowa law specifically states that innocent spouse relief will be granted if someone meets the criteria of § 6015. IOWA ADMIN CODE r. 701-38.15 (422).

---

[1] *See* Ind. Dep't Revenue, *Annual Public Hearing Meeting Minutes* (2019), *available at* https://www.in.gov/dor/files/2019-annual-public-hearing-minutes.pdf (last accessed January 10, 2022).

17. ***Kansas***

Kansas law has a provision entitled "Federal Innocent Spouse Rule Conformity," which mandates that a taxpayer will be entitled to relief on their joint income tax return if they received relief on their federal return. KAN. STAT. ANN. § 79-32,209.

18. ***Kentucky***

Kentucky allows a taxpayer relief from joint liability if either they obtained federal relief or would have qualified for federal relief if they also had a federal liability for the same tax year. KY. REV. STAT. ANN. § 141.180.

19. ***Louisiana***

Louisiana has a specifically designated "Innocent Spouse Rule" in its tax code. Its general rule only applies to understatements and closely tracks I.R.C. § 6015(b) relief. Consistent with this approach, it must be requested within two years after the commencement of collection activity. Louisiana also has a separate provision providing for proportional relief in situations where someone would otherwise qualify for relief, but may have had knowledge of the understatement. In those circumstances, the taxpayer can still be relieved of liability proportionate to the extent to which they did not know of the understatement. Furthermore, a person can seek relief past the two year statute of limitations provided (1) that they had little or no involvement in preparing the return and did not know or have no reason to know of the understatement, or they were mentally or physically forced to sign the return, and (2) that the facts and circumstances would make it inequitable to hold the taxpayer liable. LA. STAT. ANN. § 101(B)(7).

NOTE: Louisiana is a community property state and so, in the context of seeking federal relief, an applicant may apply for relief under I.R.C. § 66 (c).

20. ***Maine***

Maine law simply defines an "Innocent Spouse" as "one who meets the qualifications for relief under Section 6015 of the Code." The statute clarifies that state relief can be given even if the taxpayer did not apply for federal relief, so long as the criteria are met. ME. REV. STAT. 36 § 5287.

21. ***Maryland***

Maryland does not have provisions for relief from joint income tax liability. However, the compromise process may provide relief. *See* Md. Code Ann. Tax-Gen. § 13-816(c).

22. *Massachusetts*

The relevant Massachusetts statute tracks the three types of federal relief available. The Massachusetts Department of Revenue requires that a request for relief be submitted as part of a Massachusetts application for abatement. It also requires that the application be accompanied by the federal Form 8857. Mass. Gen. L. Ch. 62C § 84.

23. *Michigan*

Michigan does not have a statutory provision for relief from joint liability. However, the Revenue Administrative Bulletin from its Department of Treasury states that it will follow the federal standards for relief provided in § 6015. MICHTAXGD RAB 2000-9.

24. *Minnesota*

Minnesota regulations provide for relief from joint liability if a taxpayer has already qualified for federal "b" relief or if they meet a state statutory provision that tracks the requirements of federal "c" relief. Minn. Admin. R. 8160.0500.

25. *Mississippi*

Mississippi law allows a taxpayer relief from joint liability if they obtained federal relief under § 6015. Miss. Code Ann. § 27-7-31.

26. *Missouri*

Missouri law allows a taxpayer relief from joint liability if they obtained federal relief under § 6015. Mo. Ann. Stat. § 136.303.

27. *Montana*

Montana law allows a taxpayer relief from joint liability if they obtained federal relief under § 6015. It also states that relief under state law cannot exceed the amount of federal relief granted. Mont. Code Ann. § 15-30-2646.

28. *Nebraska*

Nebraska does not have provisions for relief from joint income tax liability.

29. *Nevada*

Nevada has no personal income tax.

30. *New Hampshire*

New Hampshire has no personal income tax.

31. ***New Jersey***

New Jersey does not have provisions for relief from joint income tax liability.

32. ***New Mexico***

New Mexico law provides that if a taxpayer has received federal relief from joint and several liability, then they will also be granted state relief. If federal relief has not been granted, then the state will evaluate the claim based on the following New Mexico specific set of factors:

(1) whether the spouse had knowledge of the tax liability at the time the liability arose;
(2) whether the spouse had a meaningful opportunity to contest the assessment of tax at the time the assessment was made;
(3) whether the spouse cooperated with the department in collection and compliance efforts, to the extent the spouse had knowledge of collection and compliance efforts;
(4) whether the state can protect its interests without pursuing active collection efforts against the spouse, including collection efforts against the taxpayer;
(5) whether the spouse benefited from the transfer of income, receipts or significant amounts of property from the taxpayer;
(6) whether the spouse participated in the business and financial decisions of the household during the periods when the tax liability arose;
(7) whether the spouse participated in operating a business with the taxpayer;
(8) whether the spouse had responsibility for the finances of a business for which the spouse participated;
(9) whether the spouse had responsibility for payment of taxes for a business for which the spouse participated; and
(10) whether the spouse knew that the taxpayer engaged in business.

N.M. Stat. Ann. § 7-1-17.1.

NOTE: New Mexico is a community property state and so, in the context of seeking federal relief, an applicant may apply for relief under I.R.C. § 66 (c).

33. ***New York***

New York incorporates § 6015 into its state law. If a taxpayer seeking relief has already received federal relief, then there is a rebuttable presumption that they are also qualified for state relief. N.Y. Tax Law § 654.

34. ***Nevada***

Nevada has no personal income tax.

35. ***North Carolina***

For joint returns filed for tax years before January 1, 2018, North Carolina allows innocent spouse relief for those granted federal relief under I.R.C. § 6015, but only if there was a substantial understatement attributable to the other spouse. For returns filed for tax years after January 1, 2018, the substantial understatement requirement is removed and North Carolina will grant relief if someone has been granted § 6015 relief by the IRS for the same tax year. N.C. Gen. Stat. Ann. § 105-153.8(e).

36. ***North Dakota***

North Dakota does not have provisions for relief from joint income tax liability.

37. ***Ohio***

Ohio law will recognize as an "innocent spouse" a taxpayer who has received relief under § 6015. To obtain the advantage of this provision, a taxpayer must apply for an Offer in Compromise. Their innocent spouse status will then create a rebuttable presumption in favor of the taxpayer that they are not responsible for computations of tax arising from items attributable to the non-innocent spouse. Ohio Rev. Code Ann. § 5703.06.

38. ***Oklahoma***

Oklahoma law allows a taxpayer relief from joint liability if they either obtained federal relief or would have qualified for federal relief if they also had a federal liability for the same tax year. Okla. Stat. Ann. 68 § 2361.

39. ***Oregon***

Oregon law provides that if a taxpayer has received federal relief from joint and several liability, then they will also be granted state relief. If federal relief has not been granted, then the state will evaluate the state claim based on rules adopted by its Department of Revenue, which is in turn instructed to consider the federal factors for relief. Or. Rev. Stat. Ann. § 316.369.

40. *Pennsylvania*

Pennsylvania's statute provides that a taxpayer may seek relief if they would qualify for relief under the criteria that would allow federal "b" or "c" relief. 72 PA. STAT. ANN. § 3310-212.

Additionally, Pennsylvania has a regulation that allows the consideration of equitable relief, but its factors are slightly different than the equitable relief factors found in Rev. Proc. 2013-34. For example, "abuse" is an independent factor, although it also specifically mitigates the "knowledge" factor. 61 PA. CODE § 119.30(e)(3)(ii).

41. *Rhode Island*

Rhode Island does not have provisions for relief from joint income tax liability.

42. *South Carolina*

The South Carolina Income Tax Act simplifies the state's tax structure by adopting the federal Internal Revenue Code except for a list of provisions specifically listed as "not adopted by the State." S.C. CODE ANN. § 12-6-50. § 6015 is not listed as being excluded and so under South Carolina law a taxpayer would qualify for innocent spouse relief if they qualify for federal relief.

43. *South Dakota*

South Dakota has no personal income tax.

44. *Tennessee*

Tennessee has no personal income tax.

45. *Texas*

Texas has no personal income tax.

46. *Utah*

The Utah State Tax Commission provides innocent spouse relief if relief was granted by the federal government *only* under I.R.C. § 6015(b) for the same tax year. Applicants must file state form TC-8857, or the IRS Form 8857 along with proof of federal "b-relief." Utah, however, does not provide refunds for state tax already paid on the years in question. UTAH CODE ANN. §§ 59-10-102; 59-10-115.

47. ***Vermont***

Vermont does not have statutory provisions for relief from joint income tax liability. However, the Commissioner of the Department of Taxes can waive or reduce taxes if the reasons for this action are recorded. 32 V.S.A. § 3201(a)(5). Vermont has an informal practice of considering relief after federal relief is granted. Vermont Taxpayer Advocate, *2013 Annual Taxpayer Advocate Report* 11, https://tax.vermont.gov/sites/tax/files/documents/285761.pdf [https://perma.cc/9FMV-WD3F].

48. ***Virginia***

Virginia does not have provisions for relief from joint income tax liability.

49. ***Washington***

Washington has no personal income tax.

50. ***West Virginia***

West Virginia allows a limited form of spousal relief similar to I.R.C. § 6015(b) relief. Provided there is a substantial understatement of tax on a joint state return attributable to only one spouse and that the other spouse had no knowledge of the understatement, and taking into account the facts and circumstances, West Virginia may grant relief. W. Va. Code § 11-10-11(k).

51. ***Wisconsin***

Wisconsin allows for obtaining relief from joint liability "in the manner specified in section 6015 (a) to (d) and (f) of the Internal Revenue Code." However, the law qualifies that provision to specify that relief can only be sought within two years of the start of collections. Wis. Stat. Ann. § 71.10(6)(a)-(e).

NOTE: Wisconsin is a community property state and so, in the context of seeking federal relief, an applicant may apply for relief under I.R.C. § 66 (c).

52. ***Wyoming***

Wyoming has no personal income tax.

Appendix A: Rev. Proc. 2013-14

Part III. Administrative, Procedural, and Miscellaneous

26 CFR 601.105: Examination of returns and claims for refund, credit, or abatement; determination of correct liability.
(Also: sections 66, 6015)

Rev. Proc. 2013–34

SECTION 1. PURPOSE AND SCOPE

.01 *Purpose*. This revenue procedure provides guidance for a taxpayer seeking equitable relief from income tax liability under section 66(c) or section 6015(f) of the Internal Revenue Code (a "requesting spouse"). Section 4.01 of this revenue procedure provides the threshold requirements for any request for equitable relief. Section 4.02 of this revenue procedure sets forth the conditions under which the Internal Revenue Service will make streamlined relief determinations granting equitable relief under section 6015(f) from an understatement of income tax or an underpayment of income tax reported on a joint return, or the operation of community property law under section 66(c). Section 4.03 of this revenue procedure provides a nonexclusive list of factors for consideration in determining whether relief should be granted under section 6015(f) because it would be inequitable to hold a requesting spouse jointly and severally liable when the conditions of section 4.02 are not met. The factors in section 4.03 also will apply in determining whether to relieve a spouse from income tax liability resulting from the operation of community property law under the equitable relief provision of section 66(c).

.02 *Scope*. This revenue procedure applies to spouses who request either equitable relief from joint and several liability under section 6015(f), or equitable relief under section 66(c) from income tax liability resulting from the operation of community property law.

SECTION 2. BACKGROUND

.01 Section 6013(d)(3) provides that married taxpayers who file a joint return under section 6013 will be jointly and severally liable for the income tax arising from that joint return. For purposes of section 6013(d)(3) and this revenue procedure, the term "tax" includes penalties, additions to tax, and interest. See sections 6601(e)(1) and 6665(a)(2).

.02 Section 3201(a) of the Internal Revenue Service Restructuring and Reform Act of 1998, Pub. L. No. 105–206, 112 Stat. 685, 734 (RRA), enacted section 6015, which provides relief in certain circumstances from the joint and several liability imposed by section 6013(d)(3). Section 6015(b) and (c) specify two sets of circumstances under which relief from joint and several liability is available in cases involving understatements of tax. Section 6015(b) is modeled after former section 6013(e), the prior innocent spouse statute, and section 6015(c) provides for separation of liability for taxpayers who are no longer married to, are legally separated from, or not living together with the person with whom they filed a joint return. If relief is not available under section 6015(b) or (c), section 6015(f) authorizes the Secretary to grant equitable relief if, taking into account all the facts and circumstances, the Secretary determines that it is inequitable to hold a requesting spouse liable for any unpaid tax or any deficiency (or any portion of either).

Section 66(c) provides relief from income tax liability resulting from the operation of community property law to taxpayers domiciled in a community property state who do not file a joint return. Section 3201(b) of the RRA amended section 66(c) to add an equitable relief provision similar to section 6015(f).

.03 Section 6015 provides relief only from joint and several liability arising from a joint return. If an individual signs a joint return under duress, the election to file jointly is not valid and there is no valid return with respect to the requesting spouse. The individual is not jointly and severally liable for any income tax liabilities arising from that return. In that case, section 6015 does not apply and is not necessary for obtaining relief. If an individual files a claim for relief under section 6015, but also maintains that there is no valid joint return due to duress, the Service will first make a determination as to the validity of the joint return and may accordingly deny the request for section 6015 relief based on the fact that no joint return was filed (and thus, relief is not necessary). If it is ultimately determined that a valid joint return was filed, the Service will then consider whether the individual would be entitled to relief from joint and several liability on the merits.

.04 Under section 6015(b) and (c), relief is available only from an understatement or a deficiency. Section 6015(b) and (c) do not authorize relief from an underpayment of income tax reported on a joint return. Section 66(c) and section 6015(f) permit equitable relief from an underpayment of income tax or from a deficiency. The legislative history of section 6015 provides that Congress intended for the Secretary to exercise discretion in granting equitable relief from an underpayment of income tax if a requesting spouse "does not know, and had no reason to know, that funds intended for the payment of tax were instead taken by the other spouse for such other spouse's benefit." H.R. Conf. Rep. No. 105–599, at 254 (1998). Congress also intended for the Secretary to exercise the equitable relief authority under section 6015(f) in other situations if, "taking into account all the facts and circumstances, it is inequitable to hold an individual liable for all or part of any unpaid tax or deficiency arising from a joint return." *Id.*

SECTION 3. SIGNIFICANT CHANGES

On January 5, 2012, the Department of Treasury and the Service released Notice 2012–8, 2012–4 I.R.B. 309, which set forth a proposed revenue procedure to update and revise Rev. Proc. 2003–61, 2003–2 C.B. 296. Notice 2012–8 also modified and clarified the criteria for equitable relief, and it eliminated the two-year rule for filing a claim for relief as set forth in Notice 2011–70, 2011–32 I.R.B. 135. Notice 2012–8 invited public comment regarding the proposed revenue procedure. A total of 54 comments were received, 45 of which were general comments either in support of the revisions, asking for assistance in specific cases, or totally unrelated to innocent spouse relief. The nine substantive comments ranged from discussing one or two discrete issues to commenting on all aspects of the proposed revenue procedure and innocent spouse relief in general. Treasury and the Service considered all comments received, and the proposed revenue procedure has been modified to take into account many of the concerns raised.

This revenue procedure supersedes Rev. Proc. 2003–61. The structure and format of this revenue procedure generally follows that of Rev. Proc. 2003–61 with the following significant changes:

.01 This revenue procedure gives greater deference to the presence of abuse than Rev. Proc. 2003–61. The Service recognizes that the issue of abuse can be relevant with respect to the analysis of other factors and can negate the presence of certain factors. This change is intended to give greater weight to the presence of abuse when its presence impacts the analysis of other factors.

.02 The timeliness threshold condition in section 4.01(3) of this revenue procedure provides that a request for equitable relief under section 6015(f) or section 66(c) must be filed before the expiration of the period of limitation for collection under section 6502 to the extent the taxpayer seeks relief from an outstanding liability, or before the expiration of the period of limitation for credit or refund under section 6511 to the extent the taxpayer seeks a refund of taxes paid. This is a significant change to the requirement in Rev. Proc. 2003–61, section 4.01(3), and Treas. Reg. § 1.6015–5(b)(1) (TD 9003), that the requesting spouse's claim for equitable relief must be filed no later than two years after the date of the Service's first collection activity. *See* Notice 2011–70. In response to a comment received with respect to Notice 2012–8, section 4.01(3)(a) refers to the period of limitation for collection as its commonly used IRS term — Collection Statute Expiration Date or CSED.

.03 The attribution threshold condition in section 4.01(7) of this revenue procedure adds a new exception in paragraph (e) to the requirement that the income tax liability must be attributable to an item of the nonrequesting spouse. Under section 4.01(7)(e) of the revenue procedure, relief would not be precluded for an item attributable to the requesting spouse if the nonrequesting spouse's fraud gave rise to the understatement of tax or deficiency.

.04 Streamlined determinations under section 4.02 of this revenue procedure now apply to understatements of income tax instead of only underpayments as under Rev. Proc. 2003–61. Section 4.02 also now applies to claims for equitable relief under section 66(c).

.05 Section 4.03(2) of this revenue procedure clarifies that no one factor or a majority of factors necessarily controls the determination. Therefore, depending on the facts and circumstances of the case, relief may still be appropriate if the number of factors weighing against relief exceeds the number of factors weighing in favor of relief, or a denial of relief may still be appropriate if the number of factors weighing in favor of relief exceeds the number of factors weighing against relief.

.06 The economic hardship factor in section 4.03(2)(b) of this revenue procedure now provides minimum standards based on income, expenses, and assets, for determining whether the requesting spouse would suffer economic hardship if relief is not granted. Section 4.03(2)(b) also now provides that the lack of a finding of economic hardship does not weigh against relief, as it did under Rev. Proc. 2003–61, and instead will be neutral.

.07 The knowledge factor for understatement cases in section 4.03(2)(c)(i) of this revenue procedure clarifies how the factor works in cases involving equitable relief under section 66(c), in addition to cases involving equitable relief under section 6015(f). Section 4.03(2)(c)(i)(A) provides that actual knowledge of the item giving rise to an understatement or deficiency will no longer be weighed more heavily than other factors, as it did under Rev. Proc. 2003–61. Further, section 4.03(2)(c)(i)(A) clarifies that, for purposes of this factor, if the nonrequesting spouse abused the requesting spouse or maintained control over the household finances by restricting the requesting spouse's access to financial information, and because of the abuse or financial control, the requesting spouse was not able to challenge the treatment of any items on the joint return for fear of the nonrequesting spouse's retaliation, then that abuse or financial control will result in this factor weighing in favor of relief even if the requesting spouse knew or had reason to know of the items giving rise to the understatement or deficiency.

.08 The knowledge factor for underpayment cases in section 4.03(2)(c)(ii) of this revenue procedure now provides that, in determining whether the requesting spouse knew or had reason to know that the nonrequesting spouse would not pay the tax reported as due on the return, the Service will consider whether the requesting spouse reasonably expected that the nonrequesting spouse would pay the tax liability at the time the return was filed or within a reasonable period of time after the filing of the return. In response to comments received with respect to Notice 2012–8, section 4.03(2)(c)(ii) provides that a requesting spouse may be presumed to have reasonably expected that the nonrequesting spouse would pay the liability if a request for an installment agreement to pay the tax was filed by the later of 90 days after the due date for payment of the tax, or 90 days after the return was filed. Further, section 4.03(2)(c)(ii) clarifies that for purposes of this factor, if the nonrequesting spouse abused the requesting spouse or maintained control over the household finances by restricting the requesting spouse's access to financial information, and because of the abuse or financial control, the requesting spouse was not able to question the payment of the taxes reported as due on the return or challenge the nonrequesting spouse's assurance regarding payment of the taxes for fear of the nonrequesting spouse's retaliation, then that abuse or financial control will result in this factor weighing in favor of relief even if the requesting spouse knew or had reason to know that the nonrequesting spouse would not pay the tax liability. Finally, section 4.03(2)(c)(ii) provides that if the requesting spouse did not reasonably expect that the nonrequesting spouse would pay the tax liability reported on an amended return that was based on items not properly reported on the original return, the Service will also consider whether the requesting spouse knew or had reason to know of the understatement on the original return.

.09 The legal obligation factor in section 4.03(2)(d) of this revenue procedure clarifies that a requesting spouse's legal obligation to pay outstanding tax liabilities is a factor to consider in determining whether equitable relief should be granted, in addition to whether the nonrequesting spouse has a legal obligation to pay the tax liabilities.

.10 The significant benefit factor in section 4.03(2)(e) of this revenue procedure provides that any significant benefit a requesting spouse may have received from the unpaid tax or understatement will not weigh against relief (will be neutral) if the nonrequesting spouse abused the requesting spouse or maintained financial control and made the decisions regarding living a more lavish lifestyle. Further, section 4.03(2)(e) provides that if only the nonrequesting spouse significantly benefitted from the unpaid tax or understatement, and the requesting spouse had little or no benefit, or the nonrequesting spouse enjoyed the benefit to the requesting spouse's detriment, this factor will weigh in favor of relief. Section 4.03(2)(e) also provides that if the amount of unpaid tax or understatement of tax was small such that neither spouse received a significant benefit, then this factor is neutral. In response to comments received with respect to Notice 2012–8, section 4.03(2)(e) provides that the determination that the tax liability was small such that neither spouse received a significant benefit will vary depending on the facts and circumstances of each case.

.11 The compliance with the income tax laws factor in section 4.03(2)(f) of this revenue procedure now provides that a requesting spouse's subsequent compliance with all Federal income tax laws is a factor that may weigh in favor of relief, instead of always being neutral under Rev. Proc. 2003–61.

.12 Section 4.04 of this revenue procedure broadens the availability of refunds in cases involving deficiencies by eliminating the rule in section 4.04(1) of Rev. Proc. 2003–61 that limited refunds in cases involving deficiencies to payments made by the requesting spouse pursuant to an installment agreement.

SECTION 4. GENERAL CONDITIONS FOR RELIEF

.01 *Eligibility for equitable relief.* A requesting spouse must satisfy all of the following threshold conditions to be eligible to submit a request for equitable relief under section 6015(f). With the exception of conditions (1) and (2), a requesting spouse must satisfy all of the following threshold conditions to be eligible to submit a request for equitable relief under section 66(c). The Service may relieve a requesting spouse who satisfies all the applicable threshold conditions set forth below of all or part of the income tax liability under section 66(c) or section 6015(f) if, taking into account all the facts and circumstances, the Service determines that it would be inequitable to hold the requesting spouse liable for the income tax liability. The threshold conditions are as follows:

(1) The requesting spouse filed a joint return for the taxable year for which he or she seeks relief.

(2) Relief is not available to the requesting spouse under section 6015(b) or (c).

(3) The claim for relief is timely filed:

(a) If the requesting spouse is applying for relief from a liability or a portion of a liability that remains unpaid, the request for relief must be made on or before the Collection Statute Expiration Date (CSED). The CSED is the date the period of limitation on collection of the income tax liability expires, as provided in section 6502. Generally, that period expires 10 years after the assessment of tax, but it may be extended by other provisions of the Internal Revenue Code.

(b) Claims for credit or refund of amounts paid must be made before the expiration of the period of limitation on credit or refund, as provided in section 6511. Generally, that period expires three years from the time the return was filed or two years from the time the tax was paid, whichever is later.

(4) No assets were transferred between the spouses as part of a fraudulent scheme by the spouses.

(5) The nonrequesting spouse did not transfer disqualified assets to the requesting spouse. For this purpose, the term "disqualified asset" has the meaning given the term by section 6015(c)(4)(B). If the nonrequesting spouse transferred disqualified assets to the requesting spouse, relief will be available only to the extent that the income tax liability exceeds the value of the disqualified assets. Even if there was a transfer of disqualified assets, the requesting spouse may be eligible for relief if the nonrequesting spouse abused the requesting spouse or maintained control over the household finances by restricting the requesting spouse's access to financial information, or the requesting spouse did not have actual knowledge that disqualified assets were transferred.

(6) The requesting spouse did not knowingly participate in the filing of a fraudulent joint return.

(7) The income tax liability from which the requesting spouse seeks relief is attributable (either in full or in part) to an item of the nonrequesting spouse or an underpayment resulting from the nonrequesting spouse's income. If the liability is partially attributable to the requesting spouse, then relief can only be considered for the portion of the liability attributable to the nonrequesting spouse. Nonetheless, the Service will consider granting relief regardless of whether the understatement, deficiency, or underpayment is attributable (in full or in part) to the requesting spouse if any of the following exceptions applies:

(a) *Attribution solely due to the operation of community property law.* If an item is attributable or partially attributable to the requesting spouse solely due to the operation of community property law, then for purposes of this revenue procedure, that item (or portion thereof) will be considered to be attributable to the nonrequesting spouse.

(b) *Nominal ownership.* If the item is titled in the name of the requesting spouse, the item is presumptively attributable to the requesting spouse. This presumption is rebuttable. For example, H opens an individual retirement account (IRA) in W's name and forges W's signature on the IRA in 2006. Thereafter, H makes contributions to the IRA and in 2008 takes a taxable distribution from the IRA. H and W file a joint return for the 2008 taxable year, but do not report the taxable distribution on their joint return. The Service later determines a deficiency relating to the taxable IRA distribution. W requests relief from joint and several liability under section 6015. W establishes that W did not contribute to the IRA, sign paperwork relating to the IRA, or otherwise act as if W were the owner of the IRA. W, thereby, rebuts the presumption that the IRA is attributable to W.

(c) *Misappropriation of funds.* If the requesting spouse did not know, and had no reason to know, that funds intended for the payment of tax were misappropriated by the nonrequesting spouse for the nonrequesting spouse's benefit, the Service will consider granting equitable relief although the underpayment may be attributable in part or in full to an item of the requesting spouse. The Service will consider granting relief in this case only to the extent that the funds intended for the payment of tax were taken by the nonrequesting spouse.

(d) *Abuse.* If the requesting spouse establishes that he or she was the victim of abuse prior to the time the return was filed, and that, as a result of the prior abuse, the requesting spouse was not able to challenge the treatment of any items on the return, or was not able to question the payment of any balance due reported on the return, for fear of the nonrequesting spouse's retaliation, the Service will consider granting equitable relief even though the deficiency or underpayment may be attributable in part or in full to an item of the requesting spouse.

(e) *Fraud committed by nonrequesting spouse.* The Service will consider granting relief notwithstanding that the item giving rise to the understatement or deficiency is attributable to the requesting spouse, if the requesting spouse establishes that the nonrequesting spouse's fraud is the reason for the erroneous item. For example, W fraudulently accesses H's brokerage account to sell stock that H had separately received from an inheritance. W deposits the funds from the sale in a separate bank account to which H does not have access. H and W file a joint Federal income tax return for the year, which does not report the income from the sale of the stock. The Service determines a deficiency based on the omission of the income from the sale of the stock. H requests relief from the deficiency under section 6015(f). The income from the sale of the stock normally would be attributable to H. Because W committed fraud with respect to H, however, and because this fraud was the reason for the erroneous item, the liability is properly attributable to W.

.02. *Circumstances under which the Service will make streamlined determinations granting equitable relief under sections 66(c) and 6015(f).*

If a requesting spouse who filed a joint return, or a requesting spouse who did not file a joint return in a community property state, satisfies the threshold conditions of section 4.01, the Service will consider whether the requesting spouse is entitled to a streamlined determination of equitable relief under section 66(c) or section 6015(f) under this section 4.02. If a requesting spouse is not entitled to a streamlined determination because the requesting spouse does not satisfy all the elements in this section 4.02, the requesting spouse is still entitled to be considered for relief under the equitable factors in section 4.03. The Service will make streamlined determinations granting equitable relief under section 66(c) or section 6015(f), in cases in which the requesting spouse establishes that the requesting spouse:

(1) *Marital status.* Is no longer married to the nonrequesting spouse as set forth in section 4.03(2)(a);

(2) *Economic hardship.* Would suffer economic hardship if relief were not granted as set forth in section 4.03(2)(b); and

(3) *Knowledge or reason to know.*

(a) *Section 6015(f) cases.* Did not know or have reason to know that there was an understatement or deficiency on the joint income tax return, as set forth in section 4.03(2)(c)(i), or did not know or have reason to know that the nonrequesting spouse would not or could not pay the underpayment of tax reported on the joint income tax return, as set forth in section 4.03(2)(c)(ii). If the nonrequesting spouse abused the requesting spouse or maintained control over the household finances by restricting the requesting spouse's access to financial information, and because of the abuse or financial control, the requesting spouse was not able to challenge the treatment of any items on the joint return, or to question the payment of the taxes reported as due on the joint return or challenge the nonrequesting spouse's assurance regarding payment of the taxes, for fear of the nonrequesting spouse's retaliation, then the abuse or financial control will result in this factor being satisfied even if the requesting spouse knew or had reason to know of the items giving rise to the understatement or deficiency or knew or had reason to know that the nonrequesting spouse would not pay the tax liability.

(b) *Section 66(c) cases.* Did not know or have reason to know of an item of community income properly includible in gross income, which, under the rules contained in section 879(a), would be treated as the income of the nonrequesting spouse.

.03. *Factors for determining whether to grant equitable relief.*

(1) *Applicability.* This section 4.03 applies to a requesting spouse who requests relief under section 66(c) or section 6015(f), and who satisfies the threshold conditions of section 4.01, but does not qualify for streamlined determinations granting relief under section 4.02.

(2) *Factors.* In determining whether it is inequitable to hold the requesting spouse liable for all or part of the unpaid income tax liability or deficiency, and whether full or partial equitable relief under section 66(c) or section 6015(f) should be granted, all the facts and circumstances of the case are to be taken into account. The factors listed below are designed as guides and not intended to comprise an exclusive list. Other factors relevant to a specific claim for relief may also be taken into account in making the determination. In evaluating a claim for relief, no one factor or a majority of factors necessarily determines the outcome. The degree of importance of each factor varies depending on the requesting spouse's facts and circumstances. Abuse or the exercise of financial control by the nonrequesting spouse is a factor that may impact the other factors, as described below. Factors to consider include the following:

(a) *Marital status.* Whether the requesting spouse is no longer married to the nonrequesting spouse as of the date the Service makes its determination. If the requesting spouse is still married to the nonrequesting spouse, this factor is neutral. If the requesting spouse is no longer married to the nonrequesting spouse, this factor will weigh in favor of relief. For purposes of this section, a requesting spouse will be treated as being no longer married to the nonrequesting spouse only in the following situations:

(i) The requesting spouse is divorced from the nonrequesting spouse,

(ii) The requesting spouse is legally separated from the nonrequesting spouse under applicable state law,

(iii) The requesting spouse is a widow or widower and is not an heir to the nonrequesting spouse's estate that would have sufficient assets to pay the tax liability, or

(iv) The requesting spouse has not been a member of the same household as the nonrequesting spouse at any time during the 12-month period ending on the date the Service makes its determination. For these purposes, a temporary absence (*e.g.*, due to incarceration, illness, business, military service, or education) is not considered separation if the absent spouse is expected to return to the household. See Treas. Reg. § 1.6015–3(b)(3)(i). A requesting spouse is a member of the same household as the nonrequesting spouse for any period in which the spouses maintain the same residence.

(b) *Economic hardship.* Whether the requesting spouse will suffer economic hardship if relief is not granted. For purposes of this factor, an economic hardship exists if satisfaction of the tax liability in whole or in part will cause the requesting spouse to be unable to pay reasonable basic living expenses. Whether the requesting spouse will suffer economic hardship is determined based on rules similar to those provided in Treas. Reg. § 301.6343–1(b)(4), and the Service will take into consideration a requesting spouse's current income and expenses and the requesting spouse's assets. In determining the requesting spouse's reasonable basic living expenses, the Service will consider whether the requesting spouse shares expenses or has expenses paid by another individual (such as a family member, including a current spouse). If denying relief from the joint and several liability will cause the requesting spouse to suffer economic hardship, this factor will weigh in favor of relief. If denying relief from the joint and several liability will not cause the requesting spouse to suffer economic hardship, this factor will be neutral.

In determining whether the requesting spouse would suffer economic hardship if relief is not granted, the Service will compare the requesting spouse's income to the Federal poverty guidelines (as updated periodically in the Federal Register by the U.S. Department of Health and Human Services under the authority of 42 U.S.C. § 9902(2)) for the requesting spouse's family size and will determine by how much, if at all, the requesting spouse's monthly income exceeds the spouse's reasonable basic monthly living expenses. This factor will weigh in favor of relief if the requesting spouse's income is below 250% of the Federal poverty guidelines, unless the requesting spouse has assets out of which the requesting spouse can make payments towards the tax liability and still adequately meet the requesting spouse's reasonable basic living expenses. If the requesting spouse's income exceeds 250% of the Federal poverty guidelines, this factor will still weigh in favor of relief if the requesting spouse's monthly income exceeds the requesting spouse's reasonable basic monthly living expenses by $300 or less, unless the requesting spouse has assets out of which the requesting spouse can make payments towards the tax liability and still adequately meet the requesting spouse's reasonable basic living expenses. If the requesting spouse's income exceeds 250% of the Federal poverty guidelines and monthly income exceeds monthly expenses by more than $300, or if the requesting spouse qualifies under either standard but has sufficient assets to make payments towards the tax liability and still adequately meet the requesting spouse's reasonable basic living expenses, the Service will consider all facts and circumstances (including the size of the requesting spouse's household) in determining whether the requesting spouse would suffer economic hardship if relief is not granted. If the requesting spouse is deceased, this factor is neutral.

(c) *Knowledge or reason to know.*

(i) *Understatement cases.*

(A) *Section 6015(f) cases.* Whether the requesting spouse knew or had reason to know of the item giving rise to the understatement or deficiency as of the date the joint return (including a joint amended return) was filed, or the date the requesting spouse reasonably believed the joint return was filed. If the requesting spouse did not know and had no reason to know of the item giving rise to the understatement, this factor will weigh in favor of relief. If the requesting spouse knew or had reason to know of the item giving rise to the understatement, this factor will weigh against relief. Actual knowledge of the item giving rise to the understatement or deficiency will not be weighed more heavily than any other factor. Depending on the facts and circumstances, if the requesting spouse was abused by the nonrequesting spouse (as described in section 4.03(2)(c)(iv)), or the nonrequesting spouse maintained control of the household finances by restricting the requesting spouse's access to financial information, and because of the abuse or financial control, the requesting spouse was not able to challenge the treatment of any items on the joint return for fear of the nonrequesting spouse's retaliation, this factor will weigh in favor of relief even if the requesting spouse knew or had reason to know of the items giving rise to the understatement or deficiency.

(B) *Section 66(c) cases.* Whether the requesting spouse knew or had reason to know of an item of community income properly includible in gross income, which, under the rules contained in section 879(a), would be treated as the income of the nonrequesting spouse.

(ii) *Underpayment cases.* In the case of an income tax liability that was properly reported but not paid, whether, as of the date the return was filed or the date the requesting spouse reasonably believed the return was filed, the requesting spouse knew or had reason to know that the nonrequesting spouse would not or could not pay the tax liability at that time or within a reasonable period of time after the filing of the return. This factor will weigh in favor of relief if the requesting spouse reasonably expected the nonrequesting spouse to pay the tax liability reported on the return. A reasonable expectation of payment will be presumed if the spouses submitted a request for an installment agreement to pay the tax reported as due on the return. To benefit from the presumption, the request for an installment agreement must be filed by the later of 90 days after the due date for payment of the tax, or 90 days after the return was filed. The request must detail the plan for paying the tax, interest, and penalties, satisfy the liability within a reasonable time, and it must not be unreasonable for the requesting spouse to believe that the nonrequesting spouse will be able to make the payments contemplated in the requested installment agreement.

This factor will weigh against relief if, based on the facts and circumstances of the case, it was not reasonable for the requesting spouse to believe that the nonrequesting spouse would or could pay the tax liability shown on the return. For example, if prior to the return being filed, or the date the requesting spouse reasonably believed the return was filed, the requesting spouse knew of the nonrequesting spouse's prior bankruptcies, financial difficulties, or other issues with the Service or other creditors, or was otherwise aware of difficulties in timely paying bills, then this factor will generally weigh against relief.

Depending on the facts and circumstances, if the requesting spouse was abused by the nonrequesting spouse (as described in section 4.03(2)(c)(iv)), or the nonrequesting spouse maintained control of the household finances by restricting the requesting spouse's access to financial information, and because of the abuse or financial control, the requesting spouse was not able to question the payment of the taxes reported as due on the return or challenge the nonrequesting spouse's assurance regarding payment of the taxes for fear of the nonrequesting spouse's retaliation, this factor will weigh in favor of relief even if the requesting spouse knew or had reason to know about the nonrequesting spouse's intent or ability to pay the taxes due.

With respect to an underpayment of tax on an amended return that reports a liability based on items not properly reported on the original return, the initial inquiry is whether, as of the date the amended return was filed, or the date the requesting spouse reasonably believed the amended return was filed, the requesting spouse reasonably expected that the nonrequesting spouse would pay the tax within a reasonable period of time. If so, this factor will weigh in favor of relief. However, if it was not reasonable for the requesting spouse to expect that the nonrequesting spouse would pay the tax, the requesting spouse's knowledge or reason to know of the understatement on the original return will also be considered. If the requesting spouse knew or had reason to know of the item giving rise to the understatement on the original return, then this factor will weigh against relief. If the requesting spouse did not know or have reason to know of the item, then this factor will weigh in favor of relief.

(iii) *Reason to know.* The facts and circumstances that are considered in determining whether the requesting spouse had reason to know of an understatement, or reason to know whether the nonrequesting spouse could or would pay the reported tax liability, include, but are not limited to, the requesting spouse's level of education, any deceit or evasiveness of the nonrequesting spouse, the requesting spouse's degree of involvement in the activity generating the income tax liability, the requesting spouse's involvement in business or household financial matters, the requesting spouse's business or financial expertise, and any lavish or unusual expenditures compared with past spending levels.

(iv) *Abuse by the nonrequesting spouse.* For purposes of this revenue procedure, if the requesting spouse establishes that he or she was the victim of abuse (not amounting to duress, see Treas. Reg. § 1.6015–1(b)), then depending on the facts and circumstances of the requesting spouse's situation, the abuse may result in certain factors weighing in favor of relief when otherwise the factor may have weighed against relief. Abuse comes in many forms and can include physical, psychological, sexual, or emotional abuse, including efforts to control, isolate, humiliate, and intimidate the requesting spouse, or to undermine the requesting spouse's ability to reason independently and be able to do what is required under the tax laws. All the facts and circumstances are considered in determining whether a requesting spouse was abused. The impact of a nonrequesting spouse's alcohol or drug abuse is also considered in determining whether a requesting spouse was abused. Depending on the facts and circumstances, abuse of the requesting spouse's child or other family member living in the household may constitute abuse of the requesting spouse.

(d) *Legal obligation.* Whether the requesting spouse or the nonrequesting spouse has a legal obligation to pay the outstanding Federal income tax liability. For purposes of this factor, a legal obligation is an obligation arising from a divorce decree or other legally binding agreement. This factor will weigh in favor of relief if the nonrequesting spouse has the sole legal obligation to pay the outstanding income tax liability pursuant to a divorce decree or agreement. This factor, however, will be neutral if the requesting spouse knew or had reason to know, when entering into the divorce decree or agreement, that the nonrequesting spouse would not pay the income tax liability. This factor will weigh against relief if the requesting spouse has the sole legal obligation. The fact that the nonrequesting spouse has been relieved of liability for the taxes at issue as a result of a discharge in bankruptcy is disregarded in determining whether the requesting spouse has the sole legal obligation. This factor will be neutral if, based on an agreement or consent order, both spouses have a legal obligation to pay the outstanding income tax liability, the spouses are not separated or divorced, or the divorce decree or agreement is silent as to any obligation to pay the outstanding income tax liability.

(e) *Significant benefit.* Whether the requesting spouse significantly benefitted from the unpaid income tax liability or understatement. See Treas. Reg. § 1.6015–2(d). A significant benefit is any benefit in excess of normal support. For example, if the requesting spouse enjoyed the benefits of a lavish lifestyle, such as owning luxury assets and taking expensive vacations, this factor will weigh against relief. If, however, the nonrequesting spouse controlled the household and business finances or there was abuse (as described in section 4.03(2)(c)(iv)) such that the nonrequesting spouse made the decision on spending funds for a lavish lifestyle, then this mitigates this factor so that it is neutral. If only the nonrequesting spouse significantly benefitted from the unpaid tax or understatement, and the requesting spouse had little or no benefit, or the nonrequesting spouse enjoyed the benefit to the requesting spouse's detriment, this factor will weigh in favor of relief. If the amount of unpaid tax or understatement was small such that neither spouse received a significant benefit, then this factor is neutral. Whether the amount of unpaid tax or understatement is small such that neither spouse received a significant benefit will vary depending on the facts and circumstances of each case.

(f) *Compliance with income tax laws.* Whether the requesting spouse has made a good faith effort to comply with the income tax laws in the taxable years following the taxable year or years to which the request for relief relates.

(i) If the requesting spouse is compliant for taxable years after being divorced from the nonrequesting spouse, then this factor will weigh in favor of relief. If the requesting spouse is not compliant, then this factor will weigh against relief. If the requesting spouse made a good faith effort to comply with the tax laws but was unable to fully comply, then this factor will be neutral. For example, if the requesting spouse timely filed an income tax return but was unable to fully pay the tax liability due to the requesting spouse's poor financial or economic situation after the divorce, then this factor will be neutral.

(ii) If the requesting spouse remains married to the nonrequesting spouse, whether or not legally separated or living apart, and continues to file joint returns with the nonrequesting spouse after requesting relief, then this factor will be neutral if the joint returns are compliant with the tax laws, but will weigh against relief if the returns are not compliant.

(iii) If the requesting spouse remains married to the nonrequesting spouse but files separate returns, this factor will weigh in favor of relief if the requesting spouse is compliant with the tax laws and will weigh against relief if the requesting spouse is not compliant with the tax laws. If the requesting spouse made a good faith effort to comply with the tax laws but was unable to fully comply, then this factor will be neutral. For example, if the requesting spouse timely filed an income tax return but was unable to fully pay the tax liability due to the requesting spouse's poor financial or economic situation as a result of being separated or living apart from the nonrequesting spouse, then this factor will be neutral.

(g) *Mental or physical health.* Whether the requesting spouse was in poor physical or mental health. This factor will weigh in favor of relief if the requesting spouse was in poor mental or physical health at the time the return or returns for which the request for relief relates were filed (or at the time the requesting spouse reasonably believed the return or returns were filed), or at the time the requesting spouse requested relief. The Service will consider the nature, extent, and duration of the condition, including the ongoing economic impact of the illness. If the requesting spouse was in neither poor physical nor poor mental health, this factor is neutral.

.04. *Refunds.* In both understatement and underpayment cases, a requesting spouse is eligible for a refund of separate payments made by the requesting spouse after July 22, 1998, if the requesting spouse establishes that the funds used to make the payment for which a refund is sought were provided by the requesting spouse. A requesting spouse is not eligible for refunds of payments made with the joint return, joint payments, or payments that the nonrequesting spouse made. A requesting spouse, however, may be eligible for a refund of the requesting spouse's portion of the requesting and nonrequesting spouse's joint overpayment from another tax year that was applied to the joint income tax liability to the extent that the requesting spouse can establish that the requesting spouse provided the funds for the overpayment. The availability of refunds is subject to the refund limitations of section 6511.

SECTION 5. PROCEDURE

A requesting spouse seeking equitable relief under section 66(c) or section 6015(f) must file Form 8857, *Request for Innocent Spouse Relief (and Separation of Liability, and Equitable Relief)*, or other similar statement signed under penalties of perjury, within the applicable period of limitation as set forth in section 4.01(3) of this revenue procedure.

SECTION 6. EFFECT ON OTHER DOCUMENTS

Rev. Proc. 2003–61, 2003–2 C.B. 296, is modified and superseded.

SECTION 7. EFFECTIVE DATE

This revenue procedure is effective for requests for relief filed on or after September 16, 2013. In addition, this revenue procedure is effective for requests for equitable relief pending on September 16, 2013 whether with the Service, the Office of Appeals, or in a case docketed with a Federal court.

SECTION 8. DRAFTING INFORMATION

The principal authors of this revenue procedure are Nancy Rose and Sheida Lahabi of the Office of Associate Chief Counsel (Procedure and Administration). For further information regarding this revenue procedure contact Branches 1 or 2 of Procedure and Administration on (202) 622–4910 or (202) 622–4940 (not a toll free call).

Appendix B: Form 8857

Form **8857**
(Rev. June 2021)
Department of the Treasury
Internal Revenue Service (99)

Request for Innocent Spouse Relief

▶ Go to *www.irs.gov/Form8857* for instructions and the latest information.

OMB No. 1545-1596

IMPORTANT THINGS YOU SHOULD KNOW

- Do not file this form with your tax return. See *Where To File* in the instructions.
- See the instructions for this form and Pub. 971, Innocent Spouse Relief, for help in completing this form and for a description of the factors the IRS takes into account in deciding whether to grant innocent spouse relief. The Form 8857 instructions and Pub. 971 are available at *www.irs.gov*.
- Attach the complete copy of any document requested or that you otherwise believe will support your request for relief.
- The IRS is required by law to notify the person listed on line 6 that you have requested this relief. That person will have the opportunity to participate in the process by completing a questionnaire about the tax years you enter on line 3 (the years for which you want innocent spouse relief).
- The IRS will not disclose the following information: your current name, address, phone numbers, or employer(s).
- **Note:** If you petition the Tax Court to review your request for relief, the Tax Court may only be allowed to consider information you or the person on line 6 provided us before we made our final determination, additional information we included in our administrative file about your request for relief, and any information that is newly discovered or previously unavailable. Therefore, it is important that you provide us with all information you want us or the Tax Court to consider.

Note: If you need more room to write your answer for any question, attach more pages. Be sure to write your name and social security number on the top of all pages you attach.

Part I Should you file this form?

Generally, both taxpayers who file a joint return are responsible, jointly and individually, for paying any tax, interest, or penalties from your joint return. If you believe the person with whom you filed a joint return should be solely responsible for an erroneous item or an underpayment of tax from your joint tax return, you may be eligible for innocent spouse relief.

Innocent spouse relief may also be available if you were a resident of a community property state (see list of community property states in the instructions) and did not file a joint federal income tax return and you believe you should not be held responsible for the tax attributable to an item of community income.

1 **Do either of the paragraphs above describe your situation?**

☐ Yes. You can file this Form 8857. Go to line 2.

☐ No. Do not file this Form 8857, but go to line 2 to see if you can file a different form.

2 **Did the IRS take your share of a joint refund from any tax year to pay any of the following past-due debt(s) owed ONLY by the person listed on line 6?**

• Child support • Spousal support • Student loan (or other federal nontax debt) • Federal or state taxes

☐ Yes. You may be able to get back your share of the refund. See Form 8379, Injured Spouse Allocation, and its instructions. Go to line 3 if you answered "Yes" to line 1.

☐ No. Go to line 3 if you answered "Yes" to line 1. If you answered "No" to line 1, do not file this form.

3 **If you determine you should file this form, enter each tax year you want innocent spouse relief.** It is important to enter the correct year. For example, if the IRS used your 2020 income tax refund to pay a 2018 joint tax liability, enter tax year 2018, not tax year 2020.

Tax Year ________ Tax Year ________ Tax Year ________
Tax Year ________ Tax Year ________ Tax Year ________

Part II Tell us about yourself and the person listed on line 6 for the tax years you want relief.

4 Is English your primary or preferred language?

☐ Yes.

☐ No. If "No," what is your primary or preferred language?

5 Your current name (see instructions)	**Your social security number**	
Address where you wish to be contacted. Check here if you want the IRS to send all mail for you, including legal notices, to this address (see instructions): . . . ☐		
Number and street or P.O. box	Apt. no.	**County**
City, town or post office, state, and ZIP code. If a foreign address, see instructions.	Best or safest daytime phone number (between 6 a.m. and 5 p.m. Eastern time)	
	Check here if you consent to the IRS leaving a voicemail message at this number ▶ ☐	

For Privacy Act and Paperwork Reduction Act Notice, see instructions. Cat. No. 24647V Form **8857** (Rev. 6-2021)

Form 8857 (Rev. 6-2021) Page **2**

Your current name	**Your social security number**

Note: If you need more room to write your answer for any question, attach more pages. Be sure to write your name and social security number on the top of all pages you attach.

6 **Who was your spouse for the tax years you want relief?** File a separate Form 8857 for tax years involving different spouses or former spouses.

That person's current name		**Social security number** (if known)
Current home address (number and street) (if known). If a P.O. box, see instructions.	Apt. no.	
City, town or post office, state, and ZIP code. If a foreign address, see instructions.		Daytime phone number (between 6 a.m. and 5 p.m. Eastern time)

7 **What is the current marital status between you and the person on line 6?**

☐ Married and still living together

☐ Married and living apart since ________ MM/DD/YYYY

☐ Widowed since ________ MM/DD/YYYY Attach a photocopy of the death certificate and will (if one exists).

☐ Legally separated since ________ MM/DD/YYYY Attach a photocopy of your **entire** separation agreement.

☐ Divorced since ________ MM/DD/YYYY Attach a photocopy of your **entire** divorce decree.

Note: A divorce decree stating that your former spouse must pay all taxes does not necessarily mean you qualify for relief.

8 **What was the highest level of education you had completed when the return or returns were filed?** If the answers are **not** the same for all tax years, explain below.

☐ Did not complete high school

☐ High school diploma or equivalent

☐ Some college

☐ College degree or higher. List any degrees you have ▶ ________

List any college-level business or tax-related courses you completed ▶ ________

Explain ▶ ________

9 **When any of the returns listed on line 3 were filed, did you have a mental or physical health problem or do you have a mental or physical health problem now?** If the answers are **not** the same for all tax years, explain below.

☐ Yes. Attach a statement to explain the problem and when it started. Provide photocopies of any documentation, such as medical bills or a doctor's report or letter.

☐ No.

Explain ▶ ________

10 **Is there any information you are afraid to provide on this form, but are willing to discuss?** ☐ Yes ☐ No

Part III **Tell us if and how you were involved with finances and preparing returns for the tax years you want relief.**

11 **Did you intend to file a joint return for the tax year(s) listed on line 3?** See instructions. ☐ Yes ☐ No

Explain why or why not ▶ ________

Form **8857** (Rev. 6-2021)

Form 8857 (Rev. 6-2021) Page **3**

Your current name	Your social security number

Note: If you need more room to write your answer for any question, attach more pages. Be sure to write your name and social security number on the top of all pages you attach.

12 **Describe your involvement in preparing the returns.** Include details such as whether you prepared or assisted in the preparation of joint returns (for example, by providing Forms W-2 or 1099, gathering receipts, canceled checks, or other documentation), and whether you reviewed the returns before they were filed (and, if you did not review them, why not). If you were not involved in preparing the returns, did you agree to file the joint returns or did you know that the joint returns were filed? Explain below.

13 **Explain what you knew about the income of the person on line 6 when the returns were filed.** For example, describe each type of income that person had (such as wages, social security, gambling winnings, or self-employment business income), the amount of each type of income, and the year it was received. If that person had income you didn't know about when the returns were filed, explain why you did not know. If the person on line 6 was self-employed, explain whether and how you helped that person with the books and records.

14 **Explain what you knew about any missing information on the returns when they were filed, and whether you asked about anything on the returns that you knew was missing.** Also, explain what you knew about any incorrect information on the returns, even if you did not know the information was incorrect when the returns were filed, and whether you asked about anything on the returns that was incorrect. For example, if there was a deduction or credit on the returns, were you aware of any facts that made the item not allowable as a deduction or credit? If the answer is not the same for all tax years, explain below.

15 **If the returns showed a balance due to the IRS, explain when and how you thought the balance due would be paid.** If you didn't know the returns showed a balance due, explain why not.

16 **Describe any financial problems you were having when the returns were filed, such as bankruptcy or bills you could not pay.** If the financial problems were not the same for all tax years, explain below.

17 **Describe how you were involved in the household finances and your role in deciding how money was spent.** For example, explain whether you and the person on line 6 had joint accounts and how you or the person on line 6 used them (such as by making deposits, paying bills from those accounts, or reviewing the monthly bank statements). Explain what you knew about any separate accounts the person on line 6 had. If your involvement was not the same for all tax years, explain below.

18 **For the years you want relief, did you or the person on line 6 incur any large purchases and/or expenses?** ☐ Yes ☐ No
If "Yes," describe any large expenses you or the person on line 6 incurred (such as trips, home improvements, or private schooling), or any large purchases you or the person on line 6 made (such as automobiles, appliances, jewelry, etc.). Include the types and amounts of the expenses and purchases and the years they were incurred or made.

Form **8857** (Rev. 6-2021)

Form 8857 (Rev. 6-2021) Page **4**

Your current name	**Your social security number**

Note: If you need more room to write your answer for any question, attach more pages. Be sure to write your name and social security number on the top of all pages you attach.

19 Did the person on line 6 transfer any assets to you? ☐ Yes ☐ No

If "Yes," list the assets (money or property, such as real estate, stocks, bonds, or other property) the person on line 6 transferred to you. Include the dates they were transferred and their fair market value on the dates of transfer. If the property was secured by any debt (such as a mortgage on real estate), explain who was responsible for making payments on the debt, how much was owed on the debt at the time of transfer, and whether the debt has been satisfied. Explain why the assets were transferred to you. If you no longer possess or own the assets, explain what happened to the assets.

Part IV Tell us about your current financial situation.

20 Tell us about your assets. Your assets are your money and property. Property includes real estate, motor vehicles, stocks, bonds, and other property that you own. In the table below, list the amount of cash you have on hand and in your bank accounts. Also, list each item of property, the fair market value (as defined in the instructions) of each item, and the balance of any outstanding loans you used to acquire each item.

Description of Asset	Fair Market Value	Balance of Any Outstanding Loans You Used To Acquire the Asset

21 How many people are you currently supporting, including yourself? ______

22 Tell us your current average monthly income and expenses for your entire household.

Monthly Income—If family or friends are helping to support you, include the amount of support as gifts below.	**Amount**
Gifts	
Wages (gross pay)	
Pensions	
Unemployment	
Social security	
Government assistance, such as housing, food stamps, grants, etc.	
Alimony	
Child support	
Self-employment business income	
Rental income	
Interest and dividends	
Other income, such as disability payments, gambling winnings, etc. List each type below:	
Type	
Type	
Type	
Total Monthly Income	

Form **8857** (Rev. 6-2021)

Form 8857 (Rev. 6-2021) Page **5**

Your current name	Your social security number

Note: If you need more room to write your answer for any question, attach more pages. Be sure to write your name and social security number on the top of all pages you attach.

Monthly Expenses—Enter all expenses, including expenses paid with income from gifts.	**Amount**
Food and Personal Care:	
Food	
Housekeeping supplies	
Clothing and clothing services	
Personal care products and services	
Transportation:	
Auto loan/lease payment, gas, insurance, licenses, parking, maintenance, etc.	
Public transportation	
Housing and Utilities:	
Rent or mortgage	
Real estate taxes and insurance	
Electric, oil, gas, water, trash, etc.	
Telephone and cell phone	
Cable and Internet	
Medical:	
Health insurance premiums	
Out-of-pocket expenses	
Other:	
Child and dependent care	
Caregiver expenses	
Income tax withholding (federal, state, and local)	
Estimated tax payments	
Term life insurance premiums	
Retirement contributions (employer required)	
Retirement contributions (voluntary)	
Union dues	
Unpaid state and local taxes (minimum payment)	
Student loans (minimum payment)	
Court-ordered debt payments (for example, court- or agency-ordered child support, alimony, and garnishments). List each type below:	
Type	
Type	
Type	
Miscellaneous	
Total Monthly Expenses	

Part V Complete this part if you were (or are now) a victim of domestic violence or abuse.

This information is not mandatory. See Pub. 971 for assistance. If you have concerns about your safety, please consider contacting the confidential 24-hour National Domestic Violence Hotline at 1-800-799-SAFE (7233), or 1-800-787-3224 (TTY), or 1-855-812-1001 (video phone, only for deaf callers).

23a Were you or a member of your family a victim of abuse or domestic violence by the person on line 6? (Abuse includes physical, psychological, sexual, emotional, or financial abuse, and can include the abuser making you afraid to disagree with him or her or causing you to fear for your safety.)

☐ Yes. Complete the questions below. We will put a code on your separate account. This will enable us to respond appropriately and be sensitive to your situation.

Note: We will remove the code from your account if you request it. If you do not want us to put the code on your account check here. ☐

☐ No. If "No," go to Part VI.

Form **8857** (Rev. 6-2021)

Form 8857 (Rev. 6-2021) Page **6**

Your current name	**Your social security number**

Note: If you need more room to write your answer for any question, attach more pages. Be sure to write your name and social security number on the top of all pages you attach.

b Describe the abuse you experienced, including approximately when it began and how it may have affected you, your children, or other members of your family. Explain how this abuse affected your ability to question the reporting of items on your tax return or the payment of the tax due on your return. Please attach a written statement, if needed.

c Are you afraid of the person listed on line 6?

☐ Yes ☐ No

d Does the person listed on line 6 pose a danger to you, your children, or other members of your family?

☐ Yes ☐ No

To properly evaluate your claim, please attach copies of documentation you may have, for example:

- Protection and/or restraining order;
- Police reports;
- Medical records, including those of therapists or counselors;
- Doctor's report or letter;
- Injury photographs;
- A statement from someone who was a victim of or witnessed the abuse or the results of the abuse; and
- Any other documentation you may have.

Part VI Additional information

24 Please provide any other information you want us to consider from the years that this form is about or any other years during which you filed a joint return with the person you listed on line 6 in determining whether it would be unfair to hold you liable for the tax.

Part VII Tell us if you would like a refund.

25 By checking this box and signing this form, you are indicating that you would like a refund if you qualify for relief and if you already paid the tax. See instructions . . . . ☐

Reminder: Please attach the ***complete copy*** of any document requested or that you otherwise believe will support your request for innocent spouse relief.

Caution:
By signing this form, you understand that, by law, we must contact the person on line 6. See instructions for details.

Sign Here

Under penalties of perjury, I declare that I have examined this form and any accompanying schedules and statements, and to the best of my knowledge and belief, they are true, correct, and complete. Declaration of preparer (other than taxpayer) is based on all information of which preparer has any knowledge.

Keep a copy for your records. ▶ Your signature | Date

Paid Preparer Use Only	Print/Type preparer's name	Preparer's signature	Date	Check ☐ if self-employed	PTIN
	Firm's name ▶			Firm's EIN ▶	
	Firm's address ▶			Phone no.	

Form **8857** (Rev. 6-2021)

Appendix C: IRS Notice to Nonrequesting Spouse

Appendix C1: LTR 3284C

IRS Department of the Treasury Internal Revenue Service
P.O. Box 120053, Stop 840F
Covington KY 41012

In reply refer to: [redacted]
Dec. 15, 2020 LTR 3284C 3
[redacted] 201512 30 2
Input Op: [redacted]
BODC: SB

[redacted]

016264

Social security number: [redacted]
Form: 1040
Tax Years: 2015

Contact Person: Ms. Casey
Employee identification number: 1000197591
Contact telephone number: 855-851-2009

Dear Taxpayer:

We received a Form 8857, Request for Innocent Spouse Relief, from the person with whom you filed the joint return for the years above. This is a request for relief from a debt on a joint income tax return. You have the right to participate by giving us additional information.

If you don't respond, we'll use the information available to make a decision. If we grant relief to the person with whom you filed a joint return, you alone could be responsible for the amount owed. In addition, the amount you owe could increase if we refund amounts previously paid by the person who was your spouse.

Please fill out Form 12508, Questionnaire for Non-Requesting Spouse. Your response must be postmarked or faxed no later than 30 days from the date of this letter.

You can fax your form to us at 855-201-8013 or mail it to the address at the top of the first page of this letter. We'll notify you by letter after we make a decision. If the person with whom you filed the joint return meets the requirements for full or partial relief, you'll have the opportunity to appeal that decision.

The Taxpayer Advocate Service (TAS) is an independent organization within the IRS that can help protect your taxpayer rights. TAS can offer help if your tax problem is causing a hardship, or you've tried but haven't been able to resolve your problem with the IRS. If you qualify for TAS assistance, which is always free, TAS will do everything possible to help you. Visit www.taxpayeradvocate.irs.gov or call 877-777-4778.

[redacted]
Dec. 15, 2020 LTR 3284C 3
[redacted] 201512 30 2
Input Op: [redacted]

[redacted]

If you want to authorize a third party to represent you, complete Form 2848, Power of Attorney and Declaration of Representative. If you want to give us permission to release your confidential tax information to a third party, complete Form 8821, Tax Information Authorization.

Review Publication 971, Innocent Spouse Relief, for more information about filing an innocent spouse claim.

You can get any form or publication mentioned in this letter by visiting our website at www.irs.gov/forms-pubs or by calling 800-TAX-FORM (800-829-3676).

If you have questions, you can call the person listed at the top of this letter between 7:30 a.m. and 3:30 p.m. ET.

If you prefer, you can write to the address at the top of the first page of this letter.

When you write, include a copy of this letter, and provide your telephone number and the hours we can reach you in the spaces below.

Telephone number ( )________________________ Hours ____________________

Keep a copy of this letter for your records.

Thank you for your cooperation.

Sincerely yours,

Anthony Woodson, Senior Manager
Innocent Spouse Operation

Appendix C2: Form 12508

Form **12508**
(June 2021)

Department of the Treasury - Internal Revenue Service

Questionnaire for Non-Requesting Spouse

We recognize that some of these questions involve sensitive subjects. However, we need this information to evaluate the circumstances of the request for relief and properly determine whether relief should be given. If this form is not completed and returned, the request for relief will be considered based on the information available to us.

If the requesting spouse petitions the Tax Court to review their request for relief, the Tax Court may only be allowed to consider information you and the requesting spouse provided before we made our final determination, additional information we included in our administrative file about the requesting spouse's request for relief, and any information that is newly discovered or previously unavailable. Therefore, it is important that you provide us with information you want us or the Tax Court to consider.

Part I - Tell Us About Yourself

1. Your current name		Your social security number
Your current home address *(number & street)*	Apartment number	County
City, town or post office box, state and ZIP code		Daytime phone number *(between 6 a.m. and 5 p.m. eastern time)*

2. What is the current status between you and your spouse for the years that relief was requested? *(On this form we refer to your spouse for the years that relief was requested as that individual)*

☐ Married and living together

☐ Married living apart since ______________ *(MM/DD/YYYY)*

☐ Legally separated since ______________ *(MM/DD/YYYY)*

☐ Divorced since ______________ *(MM/DD/YYYY)*

☐ Widowed since ______________ *(MM/DD/YYYY)*

Note: A divorce decree stating you must pay all taxes does not necessarily mean that individual will qualify for relief.

Part II - Tell Us About Filing the Returns and Your Financial Situation for the Years Listed on the Letter

If the information is not the same for all tax years, explain. If you need more room to write your answer for any question, attach more pages. Be sure to write your name and social security number on the top of all pages you attach.

3. How were both of you involved with preparing the returns during those tax years? Check all that apply and explain, if necessary. If the answers are not the same for all the years, explain

You	That Individual	
☐	☐	Prepared or helped prepare the returns
☐	☐	Gathered receipts and canceled checks
☐	☐	Gave tax documents (such as W-2s, 1099s, etc.) to the person who prepared the returns
☐	☐	Asked the person who prepared the returns to explain any items or amounts
☐	☐	Reviewed the returns before filing them
☐	☐	Did not review the returns before filing them
☐	☐	Was not involved with preparing the return
☐	☐	Other

Explain, if necessary

Catalog Number 28730P www.irs.gov Form **12508** (Rev. 6-2021)

4. When you filed the returns, were any amounts owed to the IRS for those years

☐ Yes. Explain how the amounts owed were to be paid

☐ No

5. When that individual signed/filed any of the returns, was he/she aware of any financial problems you were having *(for example, bankruptcy or bills you could not pay)*

☐ Yes. Explain

☐ No

☐ Do not know

6. For those years, what kinds of accounts did you have? Check all that apply. Explain if the answers are not the same for all the years

Joint	Separate	
☐	☐	Checking or money market
☐	☐	Savings or certificate of deposit

How did that individual use those accounts? Check all that apply

Joint	Separate	
☐	☐	Made deposits
☐	☐	Reviewed bank statements or balanced the checkbook
☐	☐	Paid bills
☐	☐	Knew how much money was in the account
☐	☐	Made withdrawals from the account
☐	☐	Did not know about the account
☐	☐	Did not use the account
☐	☐	Was not involved in handling money for the household

Explain, if necessary

7. Did you ever transfer assets to that individual? *(Did you put something of value, such as real estate or stocks, in that individual's name rather than in your own name)*

☐ Yes. List the assets and the dates they were transferred. Explain why the assets were transferred

☐ No

8. During those tax years, were you self employed

☐ Yes. Explain how that individual was involved in your business

☐ No

9. If the tax year(s) in question were audited, what items, if any, changed? Were the changed items yours or that individual's? *(For example, unreported income, disallowed deductions, unclaimed credits)*

10. If the audit results changed your business income or deductions on your tax return, did that individual help you in the business? If so how? If not, did that individual know about your business affairs? Explain

11. If the items changed by the audit were yours, did that individual benefit from them? *(Example, unreported income paid for a family vacation, car, jewelry, etc.)* Explain

12. Do you have any other information you want us to consider

Sign Here

Under penalties of perjury, I declare that I have examined this statement and to the best of my knowledge it is true, correct, and complete.

Signature	Date

Keep a copy for your records. Return the original signed form and any attachments or you may fax the signed form and attachments.

Appendix D: Tax Court Petition Form

Information About Filing a Case in the United States Tax Court

Attached are the forms to use in filing your case in the United States Tax Court. It is very important that you take time to carefully read the information on this page and that you properly complete and submit these forms to the United States Tax Court, 400 Second Street, N.W., Washington, D.C. 20217, or file the forms electronically pursuant to the Court's eFiling provisions.

Small Tax Case or Regular Tax Case

If you seek review of an action (other than a whistleblower or a certification action) listed in paragraph 1 of the petition form (Form 2), you may file your petition as a "small tax case" if your dispute meets certain dollar limits (described below). "Small tax cases" are handled under simpler, less formal procedures than regular cases. However, the Tax Court's decision in a small tax case cannot be appealed to a Court of Appeals by the IRS or by the taxpayer(s). You can choose to have your case conducted as either a small tax case or a regular case by checking the appropriate box in paragraph 4 of the petition form (Form 2). If you check neither box, the Court will file your case as a regular case.

Dollar Limits: Dollar limits for a small tax case vary slightly depending on the type of IRS action you seek to have the Tax Court review:

(1) If you seek review of a Notice of Deficiency, the amount of the deficiency (including any additions to tax or penalties) that you dispute cannot exceed $50,000 for any year.

(2) If you seek review of a Notice of Determination Concerning Collection Action, the total amount of unpaid tax cannot exceed $50,000 for all years combined.

(3) If you seek review of a Notice of Determination Concerning Relief From Joint and Several Liability Under Section 6015 (or if the IRS failed to send you any Notice of Determination with respect to a request for spousal relief that you submitted to the IRS at least 6 months ago), the amount of spousal relief sought cannot exceed $50,000 for all years combined.

(4) If you seek review of a Notice of Determination of Worker Classification, the amount in dispute cannot exceed $50,000 for any calendar quarter.

(5) If you seek review of a Notice of Final Determination for [Full/Partial] Disallowance of Interest Abatement Claim (or if the IRS failed to send you a Notice of Final Determination with respect to a claim for interest abatement that you filed with the IRS at least 180 days before), the amount of the abatement cannot exceed $50,000.

Enclosures

To help ensure that your case is properly processed, please enclose the following items when you mail your petition to the Tax Court:

1. A copy of any Notice of Deficiency, Notice of Determination, or Final Determination the IRS sent you;
2. Your Statement of Taxpayer Identification Number (Form 4);
3. The Request for Place of Trial (Form 5); and
4. The $60 filing fee, payable by check, money order, or other draft, to the "Clerk, United States Tax Court"; or, if applicable, the fee waiver form.

For further important information, see the Court's Web site at www.ustaxcourt.gov or the "Information for Persons Representing Themselves Before the U.S. Tax Court" booklet available from the Tax Court.

UNITED STATES TAX COURT

www.ustaxcourt.gov

(FIRST) (MIDDLE) (LAST)

____

(PLEASE TYPE OR PRINT) Petitioner(s)

v. Docket No.

COMMISSIONER OF INTERNAL REVENUE,

Respondent

PETITION

1. Please check the appropriate box(es) to show which IRS ACTION(S) you dispute:

☐ Notice of Deficiency

☐ Notice of Determination Concerning Collection Action

☐ Notice of Final Determination for [Full/Partial] Disallowance of Interest Abatement Claim (or Failure of IRS to Make Final Determination Within 180 Days After Claim for Abatement)*

☐ Notice of Determination of Worker Classification*

☐ Notice of Determination Concerning Relief From Joint and Several Liability Under Section 6015 (or Failure of IRS to Make Determination Within 6 Months After Election or Request for Relief)*

☐ Notice of Certification of Your Seriously Delinquent Federal Tax Debt to the Department of State

☐ Notice of Determination Under Section 7623 Concerning Whistleblower Action*

*For additional information, please see "Taxpayer Information: Starting a Case" at www.ustaxcourt.gov (accessible by hyperlink from asterisks above, or in the Court's information booklet).

2. If applicable, provide the date(s) the IRS issued the NOTICE(S) checked above and the city and State of the IRS office(s) issuing the NOTICE(S): ______________________________

3. Provide the year(s) or period(s) for which the NOTICE(S) was/were issued: ______________________________

4. SELECT ONE OF THE FOLLOWING (unless your case is a whistleblower or a certification action):

If you want your case conducted under small tax case procedures, check here: ☐ **(CHECK**
If you want your case conducted under regular tax case procedures, check here: ☐ **ONE BOX)**

NOTE: A decision in a "small tax case" cannot be appealed to a Court of Appeals by the taxpayer or the IRS. If you do not check either box, the Court will file your case as a regular tax case.

5. Explain why you disagree with the IRS determination in this case (please list each point separately):

____

____

____

____

____

____

T.C. FORM 2 (REV. 11/18)

6. State the facts upon which you rely (please list each point separately):

____

____

____

____

____

____

____

____

You may use additional pages to explain why you disagree with the IRS determination or to state additional facts. Please do not submit tax forms, receipts, or other types of evidence with this petition.

ENCLOSURES:

Please check the appropriate boxes to show that you have enclosed the following items with this petition:

☐ A copy of any NOTICE(S) the IRS issued to you

☐ Statement of Taxpayer Identification Number (Form 4) (See PRIVACY NOTICE below)

☐ The Request for Place of Trial (Form 5) ☐ The filing fee

PRIVACY NOTICE: Form 4 (Statement of Taxpayer Identification Number) will not be part of the Court's public files. All other documents filed with the Court, including this Petition and any IRS Notice that you enclose with this Petition, will become part of the Court's public files. To protect your privacy, you are strongly encouraged to omit or remove from this Petition, from any enclosed IRS Notice, and from any other document (other than Form 4) your taxpayer identification number (e.g., your Social Security number) and certain other confidential information as specified in the Tax Court's "Notice Regarding Privacy and Public Access to Case Files", available at www.ustaxcourt.gov.

SIGNATURE OF PETITIONER DATE	(AREA CODE) TELEPHONE NO.
MAILING ADDRESS	CITY, STATE, ZIP CODE

State of legal residence (if different from the mailing address): __________ E-mail address (if any): __________

SIGNATURE OF ADDITIONAL PETITIONER (e.g., SPOUSE) DATE	(AREA CODE) TELEPHONE NO.
MAILING ADDRESS	CITY, STATE, ZIP CODE

State of legal residence (if different from the mailing address): __________ E-mail address (if any): __________

SIGNATURE OF COUNSEL, IF RETAINED BY PETITIONER(S)	NAME OF COUNSEL	DATE

TAX COURT BAR NO.	MAILING ADDRESS, CITY, STATE, ZIP CODE
E-MAIL ADDRESS	(AREA CODE) TELEPHONE NO.